# BEC... A CHILD

## Working with 5 to 7+ in church

# KATHRYN COPSEY

SCRIPTURE UNION
130 CITY ROAD, LONDON EC1V 2NJ

© Kathryn Copsey 1994

First published 1994

ISBN 0 86201 862 5

All Bible references from the Good News Bible (Bible Society 1976).

British Library Cataloguing-in-Publication Data.
A catalogue record for this book is available from the British Library.

Cover photography – Steve Shipman
Inside artwork – Neil Pinchbeck

Phototypeset by Intype, London.
Printed and bound in Great Britain by
Cox and Wyman Ltd, Reading.

For Philip and Rachel who invite me to enter their world
and teach me how to become like a child

# Contents

# Contents

# Foreword

I can picture them now: Simon and Louise with their young children in Zimbabwe, George and Sue and many like them in my own church – parents with children who are coming up to five. Then there are the people whose special ministry in church is among the five to seven-year-olds. I want them all to read this book.

My own earliest experience with 5s to 7s was when, as a teacher of ten-year-olds, I was told to go and take the reception class in the 'Infants' department since their teacher would be away. I knew virtually nothing about five-year-olds – though I was to know more by the end of the day!

If *Become like a Child* had been available then, I would have sat up all night reading it. As it was, I made the mistake of so many of us when we are enlisted at church to work with children. I assumed that my basic need was to think about what I would have to prepare, what I should say, what I ought to do and how I should teach. I gave far too little of my attention to discovering what these children were like, how they related to people, what kind of understanding and feelings they brought to the learning process, and what they most needed.

I suppose we scraped through together – for that one day. I was aware that there was a gulf between them and me that I could not bridge. I was struggling too hard to meet my own expectations of what a teacher of five-year-olds should be doing, so I failed really to meet *them*, the children. They were so obviously different from the ten-year-olds I was used to. I simply could not discover *how* to be like a five-year-old again, to get inside a five-year-old's skin, and yet that was what they and I most needed. I was much too leader-centred and not sufficiently child-centred.

Kathryn Copsey helps us, through this book, to get inside the skin of a five-year-old, a six-year-old, a seven-year-old. It is out of her understanding of what it means to be that age that everything else arises. So we learn not just *what* to do with these children in our groups or in our families, but *why* such approaches are necessary and effective. Kathryn has led me to see the fives to sevens in my own church with new eyes. Whether I am leading all-age worship, or listening to some of our under-eights, or simply enjoying being part of the 'family' of that church, I am going to want to share in all they have to give, enjoy their imaginative games, learn from their wonder and spontaneity, and be among their advocates. In doing so, I want to meet again the child I once was, to enjoy her and, without being childish, to 'become like a child'.

Let's set out on a journey of discovery with this book to guide us. I believe we should find that the One who became a child himself, who blessed young children, and who tells us to be like them, will be travelling with us.

**Margaret V. Old**

# THE WORLD AT SIX

Rachel sat cross-legged on the bed chatting as I waited, ready to say goodnight. She was prolonging the process – I knew that – but I have learned by experience that these are usually the most intimate, the most special times of the day, so I was reluctant to hurry her. Earlier in the evening, she had been cutting and pasting, and a few small snippets of paper were still hiding among the blankets.

'Look, Mum!' Rachel turned over a minute piece of the scrap paper. 'The.' Puzzled, I looked more closely at the scrap: the word 'the' was printed on it.

'What is "the"?' I asked.

'THE tiny paper,' said Rachel emphasising the word 'the'.

'THE warm blanket,' I responded, following her lead.

'THE bouncy bed.'

'THE cuddly teddy.'

'THE beautiful Mummy.'

'THE lovely daughter.'

We described the room with our game until suddenly Rachel said firmly, 'That's the end of the "The" game', threw away the scrap of paper and buried herself under the covers.

As I went downstairs, I felt quite overawed. I had been given yet another tiny glimpse of a six-year-old's world. It would have been so easy to hurry past it for perfectly acceptable reasons. We all do it at times:

'Come on, it's late, you've got school tomorrow.'

'Look at all these bits of paper lying around. Could you finish tidying up, please?'

'Yes, I can see that's a "the" – now will you please get into bed.'

Just think what I would have lost!

For me, this game summed up many of the qualities and characteristics of the six-year-old child. There is the focus on the *immediate*. For children in this age group 'what I am doing now' is of the greatest significance to them. I was recently enjoying a fascinating discussion, initiated by my daughter, on good people and bad people when her attention was diverted by the diving flight of a bird past the window accompanied by the sound of a low flying plane. 'Just listen to that bird, Mum!' exclaimed Rachel. Our somewhat abstract discussion paled into insignificance at the 'here and now' sight and sound of that amazing bird.

Closely linked with this is the focus on the *concrete*, on the 'what I can see, feel, touch, hear and smell now'. That tiny scrap of paper would have been a non-event for me: I probably would have simply swept it onto the floor as I made the bed. For Rachel, it was an important tangible part of her 'now' world, begging for attention.

Then there is the *egocentricity* Rachel demonstrated. Look at how she finished our game: not 'Shall we stop now, Mum?' but 'That's the end of the "The" game.' Finished! We often tend to think of egocentricity as something negative. But we shouldn't confuse it with selfishness. Egocentricity or 'me at the centre' is necessary for a child's healthy development. In order to survive, a baby needs food, security and love. In a large, unknown world that threatens to overwhelm, she needs the reassurance that *her* needs will be met, that *she* will survive. Only as trust is established and she feels secure will she be able to look outwards and begin to take on board the needs of others. As we'll discover later, this is all part of the child's emerging world and her understanding of her own place within it.

This game also demonstrates the six-year-old's *intuitive* response to life. Intuition has to do with a feeling response, a response which bypasses reasoning. Rachel didn't look at the scrap of paper and say, 'Now let's think what sort of game we could play with this'. She felt the possibility of a game at a gut level: 'THE paper' and hey presto, the game began.

Closely related to this is *spontaneity*, the ability to respond to the immediate, to enjoy life, to have fun. The adult in me says, 'No! It's too late. We'll play one of your games tomorrow.' The child says, 'Here's a scrap of paper, let's have a game.' Just like that!

This age group is brilliantly *creative*. Would you or I have had the ingenuity to create a game out of nothing but a single word on a tiny scrap of paper with only a second's thought? And 'the' is surely the most boring of all words. Then see how the unspoken rules grew and developed from it: each taking a turn, each describing the room, each using only three words: 'the' plus an adjective and a noun, and so on.

Watch a child playing an imaginary game. Wonderful worlds appear, amazing conversations take place, new languages are developed, fascinating personalities are created, impossible scenarios emerge. The world of *fantasy* which is created is a very important part of a child's development, teaching her how to use and develop her imagination and how to understand the real world. Fairy stories are an important aspect of this which we'll explore later.

And finally, a five to seven-year-old exhibits for us the quality of *wholeness*, of integration. Her thinking is part of her body, which is part of her emotions, which are part of her senses, which are part of her imagination, and so on. Unless influenced by adult evalutions, she has no hang-ups over using her body, her vocal chords, her feelings, her stories. They are a part of who she is as an individual in her own right.

## Taking time
Isn't it amazing what we can learn about our children by taking time? Taking time to watch them, taking time to be with them, taking time to listen to them, taking time to play with them, taking time to enter their world, taking time to become like a child. Our lives as adults will be immeasurably enriched by what we discover. I can also guarantee that we will learn some pretty uncomfortable things about ourselves as a result.

As you may have guessed by now, I find the five to seven age-group very special, very challenging, and very refreshing. But I am certainly not looking at it through rose-coloured spectacles. Any temptation to do that has been well put to flight by having parented two children myself, and by having worked with this age-group in after-school and holiday clubs, church groups and training groups for some twenty years. I certainly would not want to confuse the whole area of being excited and challenged by children with the sense that they can do no wrong. Far from it! But I do want to challenge some of our traditional views of children.

Through the pages of this book, I first want to help you marvel with me at the wonderful gift God has given us in children, and to be enriched by their openness and creativity. Secondly, I want to explore with you the child's innate and unselfconscious sensitivity to the world and to God: her spirituality, if you like. Thirdly, I want to share some approaches as to how we can develop and enhance this spirituality through our attitudes and through the ways in which we work with children within a church setting. I want to explore how these attitudes and approaches can help towards forming a foundation for growth in faith in succeeding years. I believe that if we can establish a child-centred attitude, then practical skills and ways of working will naturally flow out of this. We may have developed excellent practical skills, but unless we understand why, for example, this particular approach is to be preferred to that approach in a given situation, then we are not using our skills as effectively as we might. In other words, knowing the principles underlying the choice of skills means the choice will be that much better. Hence, rather than simply providing a catalogue of skills, this book explores a number of principles underlying our approach to children; for example, the way in which a child's spirituality develops, how she views her wider world, or how she relates to those in authority. The final two sections of the book then look at some practical ways in which these might be 'earthed' within a church setting.

I am not only writing for those working with children in a church context, such as Sunday group leaders or church-based club leaders. What I have to say applies equally to parents, families, day school teachers, community workers – to anyone, in short, who cares passionately about valuing and supporting children.

Above all, my prayer is that this book will challenge you to serve as an advocate of the child. Children's rights are currently widely discussed, but just understanding their legal rights is not enough. What are the emotional, physical and spiritual qualities and needs which give rise to this emphasis on children's rights?

And within our churches, our clubs, our families, who advocates for the child? Do we? Do we ensure that there are sufficient opportunities for placing the child at the top of our busy agendas? Or are we failing to recognise the gift in our midst and are we, therefore, the poorer for it? When children sense that we, as Christian adults, are acting as their advocates, and when they sense that we are genuine in our relationships with them, then they cannot help but be drawn through us to see the beauty of the Lord Jesus Christ and to grow in their friendship with him.

Above all, as advocates for the child, we ourselves grow, for we are drawn into the heart of God. We learn to look through his eyes, and in a small way to feel his pain, his anger, his joy, and his passionate love as he watches over his children.

**And These All These**
And these, all these are mine
I know each sinew of their small frames
I hear their fear of night
I watch their fun
and when they laugh, so do I
in joy I see them invent themselves
even their shyness is a delight to me
I cherish their innocence
And these, all these are mine.
And if, when I return,
I find just one who has been defiled
One desecrated by your corruption
One invaded by your lust
One chained to your perversion
One burgled of purity
One dominated by your tyranny
One diseased through your indulgence
One famished by your inequity
One reliant on your base favours
One separated from Me through
your wicked fancy,
One, who once was Mine
Then I promise
You will never see the sun again

All you will receive is darkness
it will have no end
and you will not know peace
It will be terrible and just on that day
because these, all these are mine.

*© Stewart Henderson 1989*
*Used by permission*

# PART I

# The child who challenges

– Thinking about the world of the five to seven-
year-old –

*The children always challenge me to live in the present. They want
me to be with them here and now, and they find it hard to
understand that I might have other things to do or think about . . .
I marvel at their ability to be fully present to me. Their uninhibited
expression of affection and their willingness to receive it pull me
directly into the moment and invite me to celebrate life where it is
found.*                                                        Henri Nouwen

# 1. CHILDREN, CHILDREN, EVERYWHERE

In the 1990s, we cannot fail to notice the ever-increasing emphasis on the needs and rights of children. Children are among those most vulnerable in every society. From across the world come stories of children who have been exploited, neglected, abused, tortured, abandoned, forced to fight wars, removed from families, even killed. Others suffer in ways we never hear of: in most communities children have no voice. 150 million children under 15 years of age work full-time, 100 million children live on the streets, 40,000 die each day from malnutrition. Children live in sewers, railway stations, rubbish tips, doorways, hollows in the ground. All of this puts into sharp focus Jesus' statement about the preference of the noose and the millstone: 'If anyone should cause one of these little ones to lose his faith in me, it would be better for that person to have a large millstone tied around his neck and be drowned in the deep sea', Matthew 18:6.

On a global scale, the United Nations' Convention on the Rights of a Child with its 'Charter for Children' emphasises the right of a child to survival (the right to food, clean water and health), protection (the right to be free from exploitation and abuse), and development (the right to learn, to work and to a future) – over all, the right to childhood.

In the United Kingdom, the Children Act 1989 attempted to enshrine some of the basic rights of the child in residential and day care situations and with families. Only recently, we saw the 'right of residency' aspect come into prominence as a number of children challenged in court their right to live in a context where they felt cared for and protected. 'The National Curriculum will give all children a good start to life, whether they choose further education, a career or vocational training.' So reads the blurb on the promotional leaflet my children brought home from school. Whatever we may think about the content and outworking of the National Curriculum, in theory it, too, is an attempt to respond to the educational rights and needs of children. The emergence of organisations such as Childline and Kidscape, and the ongoing work of the Child Poverty Action Group, the National Children's Bureau and Dr Barnados, to name but a few, all bear witness to a growing realisation that children have rights, that these rights are being abused, ignored, or at the very least neglected, and that a response is urgently needed.

Perhaps the most significant aspect of this is that we are not only talking about children in the two-thirds world, children living and surviving in war zones, in drought-stricken areas, in unimaginable poverty and deprivation. Nor are we only talking of

*'What about parent's rights?'*

those in our western world experiencing life at the poverty level in powerless and marginal situations. We are talking about the rights and needs of children living alongside us, of those who play with our children at school, of those we meet on the bus, of those who come to our Sunday group. True, our children are not involved in fighting guerrilla wars, nor are they sold into prostitution or abandoned (although New York has some 20,000 'throwaway' youngsters on the street, unwanted by parents). But reports of physical and sexual abuse, of physical and emotional neglect, of a lack of understanding and regard for a child's needs force us not to be complacent.

'All this fuss and nonsense about the rights of a child. Never heard such rubbish in my day. Trouble is they have too much and too many rights – that's why they turn into hooligans!'

'Children's rights? What about parents' rights? There's no support for parents these days – it's all for the children.'

'It's terrible this child abuse, I agree. But it all boils down to keeping a tighter rein on your kids, I'd say. They've got too much freedom – and all this violence they watch on television doesn't help!'

We've all heard comments like these. Perhaps we wouldn't phrase them quite like this, but probably most of us know someone who would share at least some of these sentiments. Perhaps, although we don't like to admit it, we share some of them ourselves! But what such comments *don't* recognise is that it isn't an 'either/or' situation. It isn't children's rights over and against adults' rights. Basically, our view of children is faulty: we view them as potential adults. We are waiting for and working towards the time when they will grow up and reach maturity, finished products of our training and nurturing, modelled (if we're honest) on ourselves.

But this is all wrong. Regard for the rights of children refers to our valuing them as uniquely precious individuals in the sight of God *here and now*: unique individuals in their own right. We need to accord them the same respect and consideration that we do other adults. When we ask them not to interrupt us, we have no right to interrrupt them. When they request our attention, we have no right to ignore them – we wouldn't respond like that to an adult. The difficulty is that we often do not stop to consider how we respond to children. Frequently, we respond instinctively, based on how we ourselves were treated as children, how we have come to believe we *ought* to treat a child, how we are feeling at the time – responses which may come with the best will in the world, but which do not respect the child as a person. We need to take a new look at the child.

## Thinkabout

**1** How does your local Christian community respond to the needs of children in your area?

**2** Think of ways in which as a Christian family (at home, or in the body of Christ), you can ensure that children are valued in their own right. If you can't think of any ways, why is this? What are you going to do about it?

**2. A NEW LOOK AT A CHILD**

## A gift

The first step in acknowledging a child's rights is to recognise that a child is a gift from God (see Psalm 127:3, 'Children are a gift from the Lord; they are a real blessing'). A child is an infinitely precious human being in her own right. As parents especially, we need to constantly remind ourselves that our child is not our possession. Philip and Rachel do not belong to me: they are not mine in the sense that a jumper or book is mine, not even in the sense that our dogs, Kiri and Tasha, are mine or ours. Certainly, they are 'lent' to us by God, entrusted to us to care for and look after – and what an awesome responsibility this is. But if we allow ourselves, as parents, teachers, children's workers or whatever, to lose sight of the truth that each child is an individual in her own right, made in the image of God and as such of equal importance to an adult in God's eyes – if we lose sight of this truth, then we violate a child's basic rights.

An entirely new way of seeing children can open up before us if we learn to look at children as our equals in terms of their value. Do we still have a 'miniature adult' approach? Do you recall the old Victorian portraits in which a son was depicted as merely

*'Do you recall the old Victorian portraits in which the son was depicted as merely a smaller version of the father?'*

a smaller version of the father dressed in adult clothes? He was not seen as an individual in his own right.

When my aunt died at the age of 87, we all said, 'Well, she had a good, full, healthy life. She had completed her work. She only had a short illness.' When a seven-year-old dies, we say, 'Only seven! – what a terrible waste!' Yet the 'sevenness' of a seven-year-old is as valid and as complete as the '87-ness' of the 87-year-old. Certainly, we may say, 'What a loss – such potential', but if we say, 'What a waste', we are denying the value of that child as an individual in his own right, and the gift he offered to others through his life.

A common misunderstanding in affirming the rights of the child, in suggesting that we think of the child as our equal, is that in some way we are abdicating our God-given responsibility to the child. But the two are not mutually exclusive. In fact, we would be *denying* the child's rights if we failed in our responsibility to her.

When I say to my son, 'I'm really sorry for what I said today. I didn't mean to upset you in front of your friends', I am treating him as an individual with rights equal to my own: the right to be listened to and heard, the right to receive a genuine apology, the right to respect. When I say to my daughter, 'Let's decide together how much your pocket money should be', I am treating her as a responsible individual with ideas and opinions that have an equal value to my own. When I say to my Sunday group, 'I'm finding it very difficult to hear while you're all talking at once. Can you help me work out some rules to help us handle this better?', I am showing my group that I respect and value them as individuals and I have confidence in their ability to sort out the situation on an equal basis with me.

On the other hand, if I say to my son, 'Don't make a mountain out of a molehill, you know I didn't mean to upset you'; if I say to my daughter, 'Your pocket money will be 50 pence a week and that's that!'; if I say to my group, 'We're not going to have news time any more unless you can be quieter', I am, in fact, abdicating my responsibility in terms of teaching children aspects of respect, choice and boundaries, to name but a few.

## An explorer

Five to seven-year-olds are explorers. They're exploring new abilities physically, ('Look, Mum, I can jump down five steps'). They're playing with new concepts mentally, ('I know everything because I'm a friend of God'). They're experimenting with new words, ('What does "piss off" mean?'). Increasingly, they're moving away from the home to establish their identity with their

*'What does "piss off" mean?'*

peer group ('Can I go and stay the night with Jackie?'). They are learning to adapt to a thousand and one new experiences ('We only have water to drink at school dinners'). The paediatrician, D W Winnicott, encapsulates the five-year-old's experience of exploration using the image of a safe place, an enclosure.

> We could say that he is emerging from an enclosure: the walls of the enclosure began to have gaps, and the fences became uneven in thickness; and lo and behold, the child is outside. It is not easy for him to get back inside again or to feel that he is back inside, unless he is tired or ill, when the enclosure is re-assembled for his benefit.

> *(Winnicott 1984, p 35)*

Our responsibility in working with this age group, and as parents, is to allow children to explore and to experiment, to provide them with opportunities for discovering new delights. But above all, our responsibility is to provide a safe place for them to return to when the newness becomes all too much. Within the strong child, who amazes us with his ability to recite a long passage faultlessly in the school play, is the little child who afterwards collapses on the bed in a sobbing heap, overwhelmed by his explorations.

In developmental terms, the five to seven age-group is in a transitional stage. Sometimes the five-year-old is lumped with the threes to fives, in terms of his psychological development, whilst the seven-year-old may be lumped with six to ten-year-olds. At other times, four to six-year-olds may be classed together as a group while seven-year-olds are linked with twelve-year-olds. Such variations occur depending on whether one is looking at physiological, psychological or neuro-developmental skills and so on.

The significant point to draw from these variations is the recognition that children are developing at different rates throughout this age-group. Those of us working with five to seven-year-olds in church settings are only too aware of a variation between the five-year-old virtual non-reader or emergent reader, and the seven-year-old near fluent reader. (Some of us have also experienced the seven-year-old non-reader and the five-year-old fluent reader!) Then there is the variation between the clinging five-year-old who recently started school and the confident seven-year-old, secure in a well-established peer group network.

Finally, those of us who are parents never cease to marvel at the differences in our own children at the same age. I recall that trying to persuade my six-year-old son to go and have a meal at a friend's house was all but impossible. Trying to persuade my daughter at the same age that I actually did quite a good line in evening meals at home required all my ingenuity – she loved 'playing out'.

However, despite all the variations there are certain characteristics common to nearly all five to seven-year-olds. I hinted at some of these in the introduction (a focus on the immediate, on the concrete, egocentricity, an intuitive response to the world, and so on) and we will be looking at them a little more closely. But first, one more way to look at our five to seven-year-old child.

## A teacher

'Hang on, you've got the wrong word there,' I hear you say. '*I'm* the teacher!' or '*I'm* the parent!' Well, yes and no. I'm not suggesting here that your children take over preparing and presenting your next Sunday group session, nor that your children assume responsibility for running your home and family (although such suggestions certainly raise some challenging possibilities for both you and the children!) What I *am* suggesting is that, as you explore with me some of the characteristics and qualities of the five to seven-year-old, you don't just 'know' these in your head, as you might memorise a list of facts about, say, the lesser-spotted anteater of Western Birian (eats ants, very short-sighted, long tongue, half the size of the greater-spotted anteater, and so on).

Instead, I suggest that you allow yourself to 'grow' through learning about these characteristics. Allow the child to be your silent teacher as you think through these qualities and reflect on them. As you read, picture your own children or those with whom you work and allow yourself to see in them a focus on the here and now, on creativity, on spontaneity, a sense of wholeness, and so on. If they interrupt you in the next few minutes as you are reading, stop, look, listen and reflect. Which of the characteristics are they exhibiting? What can you learn about them from it? What can you learn about yourself? How might this knowledge change your approach to them?

By and large, we tend to underestimate both the abilities and the wisdom of children in this age group. Therefore, we fail to enhance their abilities and to recognise their insight. We fail to appreciate the wonder of their God-given 'five-ness', 'six-ness', and 'seven-ness'.

## Thinkabout

**1** Think of children with whom you are involved. In what ways do you experience them as a gift to you?

**2** In what ways do you encourage children to experiment and explore? Are you able to allow them to do this?

**3** In our culture, the expectation is that adults teach children. Think of ways in which your children teach you. Do you let them?

# 3. THE CHILD IN TRANSITION

## Hurray for the here and now!

The class guinea pig had died and one of the children wrote a prayer: 'Dear God, please look after Pip, even though he eats a lot. Amen.' Visions of eternal lettuce ran through the teacher's mind!

Perhaps the best-known characteristic of this age group is the fact that they think in concrete 'here and now' terms. Not for them abstract, vague thinking, long words, long boring talks; not for them long involved explanations. No, they want something they can get their teeth into, something they can apprehend with their senses, something that relates to their everyday world.

Incidentally, have you noticed, paralleling this, how children of this age often like plain food which is kept simple and separate? The exotic concoctions which we adults like are often (though not always) too 'abstract' for them. I remember how, as a child, I always kept my custard separate from my dessert. I liked them both but wanted to keep them separate and thus 'uncomplicated'.

All of which links developmentally with the fact that it is not until a child reaches the age of eleven or twelve and is able to move away from his dependency on the here and now and begin to look at the world in terms that do not depend on observable reality, that abstract thinking starts to take place.

*However* – and this is a big 'however' – this does *not* mean that the five to seven-year-old cannot explore abstract concepts. It simply means that such explorations need to be phrased in concrete terms – and what a struggle it is for us parents or children's workers to answer questions about the Trinity, or life after death, or morality, in concrete terms!

'Mum,' asked Craig, 'Will I be able to see dead people when God makes a new world?'

Mum struggled hard to answer that question: it was certainly worthy of any theologian. But look at how it was phrased: it had to do with 'me' (a child's egocentric world); it had to do with 'seeing' (using the senses) and 'making' (a favourite five to seven-year-old activity); it had to do with a 'world' (that which impinges every minute on the developing child). The question was a perfect example of the use of the here and now in phrasing an abstract question.

In response, we as adults need to be careful that, in our eagerness to answer the question correctly, we do not overwhelm the child with information. Craig simply wanted his question answered: Mum had to remember he did not want a full-scale treatise on life after death! This is often an issue when it comes to the child's questions about sex.

A friend of mine and her daughter were sitting watching a cartoon on television. Suddenly the daughter turned to her mum: 'How does a baby get out of your tummy?'

'Well,' said her somewhat unprepared mother. 'Underneath you have three holes: a wee-wee hole, a poo hole and a baby hole. The baby comes out of the baby hole'.

'Oh,' said the daughter, satisfied, and returned to watching Bugs Bunny with no further comment. Her question had been answered and she had received all the information she wanted.

Fundamental to the way in which a child is able to understand and interact with the world is her use of her senses. If you like, these are her doorways into the world. She sees, she touches, she smells, she hears, she tastes. What an exciting way to find out about life! As one example, have you ever noticed how a child explores her world through the sense of smell? She will climb into a new car and sit and sniff appreciatively, 'Oh, what a lovely new smell!' My daughter often pulls down my head to sniff my hair. 'It has a "you" smell,' she says. Of all our senses, we as adults have the most hang-ups about smell: look at all the air fresheners, perfumes and deodorants we use. Even my husband doesn't spend time sniffing my hair – probably just as well! But for a child, that is all part of the here and now-ness of her world.

Why is it that we adults always take refuge behind words and concepts, behind our interpretation of what the world is? I wonder if it is because coming face to face with the real here and now makes us a little uncomfortable. We have lost the art of being 'real' – a quality which a child possesses to the full.

Just as a child sees her world in a concrete, observable, tangible way, so her sense of the *present*, the *immediate* is very strong. When a child dissolves into tears because it isn't possible to do this now or get this now, she isn't being unreasonable. She is simply expressing her conception of her world. Children at the younger end of the age range especially have very little concept of the passage of time. For them, time stands still or moves only slowly. 'Is half past ten before lunch or after lunch?' 'What does it mean that Nan is coming to stay next week?' Often this is more easily explained in terms of how many 'sleeps' there will be before Nan comes, or that she is coming 'the same day as you have big apparatus at school'. A sense of time needs to be built around the already known routine of the child's life.

Many children at the age of five are only gradually beginning to develop a sense of the long-term past, 'a hint of half-forgotten things', as Winnicott puts it. I am reminded of this when I come across an old toy or gift which has played a special part in our lives and say excitedly to the children, 'Oh, remember this? Do you know who gave it to you?' and they look at me blankly and say, 'No, never seen it before.' However, developing a sense of the family past in particular is very important for children and gives them a sense of their own history, their place in the family and in the world. It enables them to feel rooted and to develop a sense of belonging – so important for their sense of self-worth. As parents, we can help in this by talking about past events, by keeping alive the memories of relatives who have died, by building up stories around particular souvenirs or mementos brought back from a holiday together. Photographs are particularly good memory-builders, and the remembering that goes on when my two sit down to look at our photo albums is very exciting. From this it can follow that particular objects will come to hold strong attachments and memories for some children.

## Hurray for me!

A natural and, if we look at it in the right context, beautiful part of a child's development at this stage is her egocentricity. As I observed before, we tend to think of egocentricity as having a negative connotation. Words like 'selfish', 'stuck-up' and 'self-centred' spring to mind. Kate reaches for the biggest biscuit on the plate and we say gently, 'No dear, take the one nearest you, not the biggest!' Certainly if a child remains in the egocentric stage and is unable to complete the transition to appreciating the points of view of others, we could end up with a self-centred, self-opinionated prig!

However, egocentricity is a perfectly natural developmental stage. In infancy, the baby or toddler relies totally on the parent or caregiver to meet all her needs. In order to survive, the world must revolve around her. But, beginning first in playgroup or nursery and then as a child enters the five to seven age-group, starts school and mixes with a world beyond her own home or playgroup, she gradually learns to see the world through other people's eyes, to take on others' perceptions.

The importance of the egocentric stage is that through it a child develops a strong sense of self – of her own importance as a person. As she operates from her own point of view, she experiences that her ideas and feelings are valid, that she *can* express her point of view, that she *can* ask to have her needs met. As she comes up against other children, similarly asserting their rights, so she learns to temper her approach.

I call this a beautiful part of a child's development because in a world where children's rights are often ridden over roughshod and where abuse takes place, a child who develops a belief and confidence in her own self-worth, is a child who is developing into a whole person as God intended. Also, a child who expresses her view of her world in a personalised, uninhibited and genuine way can be refreshing – although she can also be very embarrassing:

'Are you going to give Grandad a good-bye kiss?'

'No. He smells horrible!' (reference to his recently applied aftershave!).

*'Are you going to give Grandad a goodbye kiss?'*

Be honest! There are lots of situations in which we as adults would love to respond in a similar vein:

'What do you think of my new dress?'

'Well, I think the colour is awful and those big flowers make it look like curtain material – although I certainly accept that you might like it!'

I often wonder what sense children make of the catchphrase that I still hear used around five to seven-year-olds: 'If you want real joy', (whatever that means for a five to seven-year-old!) 'then it is *J*esus first, *O*thers next, *Y*ourself last!' An adult might make sense out of it (although I wonder how it tallies with 'love your neighbour as yourself'), but it must be totally meaningless for a child. 'Why does Jesus want me to be last? I always thought children were special to him.' Or, 'Being last always means you have to wait. I don't want to wait!' Or, 'If I've got to be last, then I don't want joy.'

A final point to note is that even while a child sees the world from her own egocentric point of view, it does not mean that she is unable to empathise or 'feel' with another person at times. There is something very special about the times when I have collapsed on the couch, exhausted, and had my son or daughter disappear silently upstairs only to return with my slippers, then snuggle up beside me on the couch. No words are necessary: they are showing their ability to enter into my tiredness and care for me.

## Hurray for my feelings!

'Dad, I feel sick!'

For several days, Dave could practically pinpoint the place on the road they would have reached on their way to school when his daughter, Janine, would say that. She'd had a good night's sleep, she'd had a healthy breakfast, she had been in great spirits at home. Now she felt sick. Dave knew she didn't feel sick in the sense of wanting to vomit or running a temperature. What she was actually saying was, 'Dad, I don't feel like going to school today'. She may not have consciously recognised what was going on inside her in so many words but, as a seven-year-old, Janine was very much in touch with her feelings, and she had the ability to express them.

*'Dad, I feel sick!'*

Children of this age frequently respond to their world at an intuitive level. Bypassing a carefully thought-out, reasoned approach, they respond at an immediate 'gut' level. What they feel, they say. As adults, we tend to weigh up consequences and censor our feelings: 'Now Jan looks tired. I wonder if she'd rather be left alone. If I speak to her, she might snap at me, or I might say the wrong thing and upset her.' Then Jan's son bounces into the room, 'Hello, Mum. You look grumpy! What's for dinner?' He came, he saw, and he responded at an intuitive, feeling level. His response to his mum was based on *what* he saw, the way the situation actually appeared to him, not on what he *thought* about what he saw.

Part of what is most engaging about children is this spontaneity, this acting on impulse in response to how things appear to them. This morning, my daughter and I were sitting in bed making a birthday card for one of her cuddly animals. I cut a circular badge out of a square of card, leaving an arch shape. Suddenly this became a bridge and the characters in her storybook marched one by one across this bridge. Wow! What creative spontaneity! One of the rich moments in being with children occurs when out of the blue a child comes up, flings his arms around your neck and says for no apparent reason, 'I really like you': a genuine, spontaneous gut reaction to where he was in his world at that moment.

Part of a child's transition through this stage is learning how and when to respond in a reasoned, thought-out manner rather than at a totally intuitive level. When a child responds at a gut level, he is responding to the here and now situation, without setting it in context. Thus, such a child may see the world as a series of episodes not yet fully sequential or ordered like a narrative story. As he develops a sense of the passage of time and a sense of his own continuity, so, gradually, unconnected images are replaced by stories and the spontaneity slowly recedes to allow for a more measured reaction to take place. The reality of these unconnected images is well represented by the child who thought that the world used to be 'in black and white', because old photographs are always black and white.

Just as we need to affirm a child's sense of self-worth which is born out of her egocentricity, so we need to affirm and value a child's intuitive, spontaneous side in order to ensure that it is not submerged under an increasingly formal, rational, logical approach – an adult approach. Symbols are one important aspect of this. For a child, a symbol *is* what it represents. It is not, as it is for us adults, a sign, a word, a picture which stands for something else. For a child that sign or picture *is* the something else and therein lies its ability to evoke a powerful feeling. For a child, symbols are magical and the response of awe and wonder which they evoke is drawn from the non-rational, intuitive nature of the child.

Watch a child's face as you decorate for Christmas. The ornaments, bells, angels, figures for the nativity scene, candles – all are brought out and arranged lovingly by eager hands. 'Now turn out all the lights,' you say, 'shut your eyes and I'll switch on the Christmas tree.' You feel excited yourself, but for the child the impact is overwhelming: the spirit of Christmas is actually there in the room. Explaining the significance of bells, the fact that angels probably didn't have wings, the question over the number of wise men, the unlikelihood of the shepherds and the wise men being with Jesus at the same time ... all of that is not only totally irrelevant to the child, it actually clutters the power of the symbol with our adult baggage. The clutter will come soon enough: 'The cross symbolises Christ's atoning sacrifice for our sins and represents his great love for us'. No! The cross as a symbol of love speaks for itself far more powerfully than can our explanations to a five to seven-year-old.

Another important aspect of a child's intuitive qualities relates to the fact that, for this age-group, reality and fantasy sit comfortably side by side. And again, as with symbols, it is to the child's loss that we attempt to discount or deaden the fantasy side. If its presence is recognised and respected as part of a child's world, it will assume its rightful place as a child progresses developmentally, and the mature adult will later recapture its riches (as, for example, in the use of imagination or visualisation in prayer) without feeling a sense of inhibition or even guilt.

'Do God and Father Christmas talk to each other?' Sarah asked.

'Well, I'm not sure. I suppose they could.'

'Then if I tell God what I want for Christmas, would he pass it on to Father Christmas?' she persisted.

Sarah could have been trying to avoid writing a letter. But it is more likely that the characteristics of God and those of Father Christmas were quite understandably closely linked in her mind. What was needed was not for the adult to express strong disapproval over the link, but gradually – perhaps over the following months – to help the child to see the essential differences between God and Father Christmas.

Many parents and children's workers are rightly concerned about encouraging an unhealthy interest in the supernatural and even the occult by allowing children to read books, play games and watch television programmes which deal with magic and perverted images of good and evil. But we need to be very careful not to throw out the baby with the bath water and so deny our children the opportunity to develop and expand their own imaginative abilities.

In playgroups and nurseries, imaginative play is a fundamental part of a child's development. Through it a child learns to explore new worlds in a safe context at his own pace. As a child grows older, he is introduced to fairy stories, fables and folktales, all of which are an integral part of every country's rich cultural heritage. Certainly, magic, witches, daring deeds, princes, frogs, ghosts, spells, kings and queens all feature in such literature but, again, these are also aspects of a child's imagination. Our responsibility is to enable the child to keep clear boundaries between the world of imagination and the real world, so that a balance is maintained and fantasy and reality can continue to coexist in the child's mind.

Without fantasy and imagination, the child's world – and ours – would be incredibly bland and dull. Perhaps what is most important to remember is that imagination is a God-given gift. Jesus invited the crowds to draw on their imaginations when painting verbal pictures such as those of the lost son and the two house builders.

Writing in *Child Education*, literacy consultant Wendy Body says:

> Stories enable children to do in their imagination what they know they can't do in real life. They enjoy anything that goes beyond the everyday constraints of the world and delight in fantasy. Magical stories can make these fantasies possible within the world of the book ... Fiction is a powerful medium for allowing children to recognise and explore a whole range of behaviours and attitudes, while being safely one step removed. They are also safe because children's books are, rightly, very moral – when did you last read one where evil ultimately triumphed over good.

> (*Child Education, October 1989, p 11*)

The writer here is talking about books, but the same may be said of the games and television programmes produced for this age-group. Some may argue that the participatory and visual aspects of games and television can make it easier for fantasy to merge with reality. Others will say that such a merger happens more easily without visual stimuli. Whichever the case, a balance must be maintained. When we find – and we will all find this because a child's imaginative capacity is so powerful – that our child is convinced a wolf is going to leap out and gobble him up on the way to school if he steps on a crack, it is clear that the balance is askew, and it is time to have a good talk.

> We teach children about dangerous phenomena by showing and explaining, not concealing ... Of course we need to protect children from harm, but we can best do that by helping them to develop a sound moral baseline and minds that are questioning rather than totally accepting.
>
> (*Child Education, October 1989, p 11*)

## Hurray for the way I see things!

As a child, I remember opening the door of a cupboard that was badly balanced, causing several cups belonging to my mother's best tea service to fall crashing to the floor. I was devastated! The fact that it was a complete accident didn't help at all. For me, the consequences determined the badness of the act. But I was not in the five to seven age-range: I was nine!

There are many different theories as to the degree to which a child's moral awareness has developed by the five to seven agerange. There are those who would say that the child's moral judgement is based on her observation of reward or punishment: that the understanding of the goodness or badness of an act depends solely on its consequences, that intention is not yet important (my experience above). But what about the child who throws a rubber to another child on the other side of the room who asked for one and in doing so 'accidentally' hits someone on the head. 'I didn't mean to, Miss. It was an accident. I was trying to help.' Intention certainly features here.

Some even go so far as to say that a child actually lacks the ability to adopt another's perspective. But we have already seen that children of this age *can* adopt another's perspective: witness my children's care for their tired mother. We also see that the *intention* can feature in a child deciding whether an act is good or bad. On the other hand, the *result* can also have a bearing: to me, breaking the cups was, in itself, a bad act. Watch a six-year-old playing a game: it's fine to break the rules if you can get away with it. But Mum might come and tell you off, in which case, follow the rules rather than be reprimanded.

There is as yet no outside moral absolute. Or is there? Some studies noting children's behaviour have observed two kinds of rules: *moral*, which relate to the rights and privileges of the individual (eg, a rule about kicking another child), and *social conventional* rules which govern interpersonal behaviour in a particular social setting (eg, a school rule about washing hands before a meal). It may be all right to break the hand-washing rule, but kicking another child definitely deserves punishment.

What emerges from all of this is the fact that the five to sevenyear-old is in a stage of transition. Sometimes intention features, sometimes it doesn't; sometimes another person's perspective is taken into account, sometimes it isn't; sometimes a child appears to have thought out issues in an amazingly complex way, sometimes the response is at an unreasoned gut level. Much depends on the child's own understanding and awareness of moral issues: how often such issues are talked about at home; how much the child is encouraged to think about how someone else might see things; how often he is allowed to win 'just this one game', regardless of rules; how often moral absolutes are talked about, in other words, how often God's rules are talked about.

## Enjoying the gift

So, our five to seven-year-old is in a creative, exciting process of transition, moving out from a world in which she is the focus and principal initiator to a world where other people are valuable in their own right and whose interests must be taken into account. As caregivers, our responsibility is to provide the opportunities within which this transition can take place. Within a church setting, it is to open up new worlds to a child: worlds where Bible characters come alive and share with us their experience of God; worlds where prayer is a reality; worlds where people of all races and backgrounds are important; worlds where, through us, Jesus' love and friendship become so real that they touch the child's own life and outlook.

We will probably never know when the child has fully completed the transition. Sometimes we'll think, 'Hey, that's a real step forward!' At other times, we'll shake our heads in frustration, 'Whenever will he understand . . .' – probably rather like God does with us. But isn't this all tied up with enjoying the gift of this five to seven-year-old? He is in the process of becoming. We can, therefore, enjoy the qualities of both the under-five and the over-seven – and all that is in between. What a marvellous gift!

But how can we even begin to provide the opportunities for growth that our five to seven-year-olds need? By entering the world of the child and seeing the world through the eyes of a child.

## Thinkabout

**1** How do you facilitate spontaneity, fun and play with your children? Are there ways in which you stifle these qualities?

**2** In what ways is the Christian family able to give pride of place to its younger members?

**3** Do you as an adult encourage a child to have feelings and to express them appropriately, or are you worried by them?

# ENTERING THE WORLD OF THE CHILD

One day a father was driving his son along a windy road across a flat stretch of marshland. It had been raining. The sky was grey and angry on one side; the sun was breaking through on the other. They were both silent. Dad was miles away thinking of what needed doing that evening. Suddenly a voice piped up beside him, 'Dad! Look! We're about to drive into a pot of gold at the end of the rainbow. If we hadn't come this way we'd never have seen it.'

In order to open up new opportunities of growth for the child, we need to enter the child's world. How do we do this? Let me suggest two ways: first, we can take the time to become like children ourselves, and second, we can get in touch with our own childhood experiences. Let's look at these in more detail.

## Becoming like a child

Please note that this means becoming childlike not childish. Jesus didn't say, 'Become childish', yet many adults confuse the two. The quality of childlikeness has to do with an ability to empathise with the child because you have learned to see the world from her perspective. Childishness refers to behaviour which is petty and infantile. A child will respect you and enjoy your company if you are childlike. A child will be embarrassed by you and avoid you if you are childish.

## Time to be

First of all, we can enter the child's world by taking time just to be with a child. Get rid of your adult need of having to be 'doing' and just 'be'. Sit by a child as she sleeps. Watch her face. Watch her movements. Travel with her into her dreams. Smile with her at her delights, jump at her fears. As you watch her, pray for her, for everything about her. For several months, I periodically observed a baby boy. Many times he was asleep. As I watched while he slept, I came to understand a part of him I never saw while he was awake: sometimes peaceful, sometimes restless, revealing little glimpses of an interior world. And when the child is awake, just be in the same room. She may be busy doing something, but you don't have to be. Just be 'companionably' there.

Children love adults that are able just to be. They are available adults, and available adults are taught wonderful things by children. Watch *what* a child watches: branches waving in the wind, muddy splashes up the side of a bus shelter as traffic speeds past, a beetle crawling along the kerb. Also watch *as* a child watches: see the expression on her face, watch her fingers tracing muddy patterns, watch her absorption in what to us as adults is often of less than no interest. Listen to a child's conversation with a friend, an animal, a visitor. Listen to a child as she talks to you. Don't just hear, but listen. Follow the child's thoughts without trying to direct, rephrase, improve or teach. See her world as she expresses it and, even when the description is slow in coming or very involved, stay with it.

## Time to play

Secondly, we can enter the child's world by taking time to play with the child. This is not a case of 'I've nothing better to do for the next ten minutes so how about a game?' That is not fun. If you are bound by a time constraint, *your* agenda will dominate and both of you will be frustrated. Good play needs space, flexibility and imagination. Your playmate(s) may like to suggest a game or you may choose one together. If you play set games, play fairly. Don't always allow the child to win, but be flexible: it is not always easy to understand or see the purpose of rules at this age. Play may also be messy, out-of-doors, imaginative, lively, quiet. Whichever you choose together, don't follow your agenda when playing, follow the child's. It is far more creative, far less stuck-in-the-mud than yours would be! Certainly, you can introduce your own additions to the game, but if you are serious about entering the child's world, let the child take the lead. This will help you enter the child's pattern or way of thinking.

You've probably often heard it said that household objects allow for far greater creativity than expensive shop-bought toys. How true! The barred staircate which we used at home when the children were babies has since served as zoo, prison, mountain, climbing frame, tennis net, shop counter, etc. And I have tidied up sundry soft toys from all over the house only to discover that they are part of a very involved, wide-ranging game. I've now learned to *ask* before any extensive clearing-up operation! So give yourself a treat and take time to play with a child. For five to seven-year-olds, play is one of *the* most important ways of learning, of understanding the world, and you can't afford to miss out on learning with them.

### Time to find out
Finally, we can enter the child's world by simply finding out what a child enjoys. Your child comes in from school and says he is 'bored'. Don't forget, this usually means he can't decide what to do – not that he is weary with the world. So don't give him a lecture saying that he is too young to be bored. Instead, suggest that he explores the contents of his toy cupboard, looks at his bookshelf, turns out his cars or soft toys... Stay with him as he chooses. Each time you'll learn something new about what he enjoys and be amazed: 'However can he play for an hour with a two-inch-high spaceman and a shoebox?'

Take time to wander around a bookshop and toyshop on your own. Decide what you would enjoy reading and playing, then take a child with you and find out what she or he would enjoy. Give yourself marks out of ten for how well your choices matched. Where your choices differed, ask the reasons for the child's preference: was it chosen because of colour? because of what it does? because it looks fun? because a friend has it? because a friend says it is good? because it has been on television? Store these ideas in your mind. They might well help when you come to choose items or toys for use in some of your Sunday group activities.

Now find out which are their favourite TV programmes and videos and why. But don't stop there: spend time watching them yourself. It is often easy to be an expert on children's programmes if you have pre-school children since parents often watch with their children. But once children start school and become more self-sufficient, they tend to watch programmes on their own. It is good to reverse this trend whenever possible.

Find out what games children enjoy playing. Which are their favourites? Where do they usually play these? What do they play in the breaks at school? Are there some of these that can be adapted to use with your Sunday group? Often a familiar game can help a new child to settle in quickly, as it can take away the 'I'm new and the odd one out' feeling. Be sure to check out the words to games beforehand though: some may need to be altered for use in a church setting.

Finally, find out about the child's world by looking at magazines and books that feature children's issues. Go into your local library or bookshop and flip through material on anything from child development to song books for children, to craft ideas, to play equipment. Look at the children's sections in catalogues and see what types of clothes are in fashion, what toys are the rage. Above all, enter the child's world, and keep in touch with what is important in it.

## Getting in touch with ourselves

We were all children once, but for some of us that 'once' may be very far away – *not* in terms of years, because age has very little to do with it. No, 'once' may be far away because for whatever reasons, we may have forgotten or lost touch with our own childhood. However, it is obvious that unless we take the time to look at our own experiences as a child, and at the part of ourselves that responds like a child, we will miss out on a very important source of information about children. As we see how our past experiences affect us *now*, so we will better understand our own children and those children with whom we work.

So let's look at our own childhood. What do we remember from it? Think about your principal caregivers – perhaps parents, perhaps other relatives. Perhaps your experience was of a very strict authoritarian parent. Is this reflected in the way you relate, say, to your own children or to your Sunday group? Perhaps you were often criticised at home and felt you were always struggling to be approved of and accepted. Does this carry over into your relationships with other Sunday group leaders where you always feel you are second best and you always run down your abilities? Can a neutral comment from your vicar or minister or another leader make you feel 'told off'?

If your childhood experiences of authoritarian parenting have left you somewhat in awe of authority figures, assuming always that 'they know best', this may also affect your attitude toward your minister or vicar. If your group perceive that you are in awe of and not very relaxed around your minister, then what message are you giving to the children about being the family of God, about the 'all ages together' dimension of worship? Children will quickly pick up your reservations and will be less spontaneous themselves as a result. If, of course, your minister *is* authoritarian, then encourage him to see different ways of relating to children. Why not invite him into the group to see the children in action, and to do some fun activities with them? Perhaps no one has ever suggested this to him before!

Then think about play. Did you play as a child? With whom did you play? What did you play? Were you allowed to just be plain silly as a child, or were you taught that games always had to have a purpose and be played 'properly'? If you notice that you find it hard to let children have fun in what you consider to be a simple, 'pointless' way, this may be why. (Incidentally, it is highly unlikely to be pointless – that is our adult perception.) If you find that messy activities like foot painting or using newspapers are difficult for you, it may be that you were taught as a child that making a mess was wrong. Don't worry! You can gradually 'unlearn' your childhood patterns. Children are often the best teachers here: just see how much fun they can have, the messier the better.

Perhaps you find it difficult to include games in your Sunday group and feel just slightly guilty and embarrassed when they are suggested. This could well relate back to a childhood injunction which said that church should have nothing to do with fun or pleasure. As a missionary child, I was not allowed to play with my Japanese friends on a Sunday. Whatever the pros and cons of this rule in our situation, I still find Sundays a hard day, a day with 'shoulds' and 'oughts' hanging over it.

So over all, how well do we remember our childhood? Do we

*'If you find that messy activities like foot painting are
difficult for you, don't worry!'*

have good or painful memories? Can we recapture any 'feelings' from childhood? Sometimes a picture, a song, a smell will be enough to bring a childhood experience to mind. Does the following extract from the poem 'Is there a lost child in you?' by Sister Macrina Wiederkehr ring true for you?

> There are days
> when
> my adult ways
> turn tasteless in my mouth
> and the child of long ago
> starts
> pressing on my soul.
>
> On days like that
> I long to touch that child again
> and let her take me by the hand
> and lead me down
> a path that has a heart
> and show me all the things
> that
> I've stopped seeing
> because I've grown
> too tall.

*(Wiederkehr 1990, p 62)*

Some of our strongest memories may be related to joy: moments of feeling secure, appreciated, valued, loved. Others, equally strong, may be related to guilt and sadness: a memory of being in the way, of not being wanted, of not being heard. As you recall these memories, ask yourself: where do I experience these same feelings now? In what situations? Because how we are now will inevitably affect the way we relate to children and the way we understand them. If our memories are those of having been listened to and valued, then the chances are that we, in turn, will relate to children in the same way. If, however, we find that our childhood has left us with painful memories, we may experience the same feelings now, making it difficult for us to relate fully to our children.

Perhaps you have never thought of understanding children by looking at your own childhood and your response to children now. But what better place to begin than with your own first-hand experiences? These are unique to you, and understanding them can only increase your empathy with and sensitivity to children. In his book, *Pastoral Care with Children in Crisis*, Andrew Lester makes a similar point as he notes the personal preparations that a pastor needs to make if he is to deal effectively with children in a crisis situation:

> Caring for children effectively includes the willingness to identify with the child's hurt, vulnerability, fear, anger, and sense of loss. To empathise with the child, to 'hang in there' in the face of his or her pain, can only be managed if you have been willing to claim your own personal pain. You must be willing to explore personal experiences with grief, loss, guilt, shame, fear, and danger, particularly if experienced as a child. If wounds from the past are left unhealed, it will be difficult for you to allow a child to deal openly with a crisis in your presence. The child's emotional pain will be too threatening to that which lies unresolved in one of your interior closets.
>
> (*Lester 1985, p 80–1*)

The basic point he is making here is that, in order to empathise with a child's pain (or joy), we need to be aware of the things that have happened to us in the past that make us unable to empathise. For example, perhaps as a child we might have experienced a great loss of love (divorce, separation, death, parents too busy). If this was painful for us, we may have seen it as our fault and may have avoided thinking about it, even consciously forgotten it. As a result, we may find it difficult to empathise with a child going through a similar experience. It may well be necessary for us to explore that childhood experience within a loving, caring setting with a supportive friend, before we are able to empathise with the child.

That's all very well, you may say, but we are not primarily dealing with children at a crisis stage. Perhaps that may be true for you, but the principle applies equally to dealing with all aspects of childhood which touch us personally. To rephrase Andrew Lester's first sentence: 'Caring for children effectively also includes a willingness to identify with the child's joy, wonder, vulnerability, dreams and humour as well as with his or her fear, anger and sense of loss.' Are we able to identify with all these aspects of the child's world? We may well find that this can be done most effectively if we have already looked at our own childhood experiences in these areas.

## Thinkabout

1 Think back to your own childhood. Are there any ways in which your own experiences as a child make it difficult for you to enter into the child's world?

2 Do you have enough time in your life for play? What does play mean to you?

3 When did you last sit down and play a game, explore a toy shop, read a children's book, or watch a children's video or television programme?

# 5. GIFTS FOR THE CHILD

What, then, does the child need from us? There are three invaluable gifts we can give a child: the gift of being valued, the gift of being listened to and the gift of being accepted unconditionally. As Christian parents, caregivers, club leaders, Sunday group leaders, we are uniquely suited to giving these gifts to our children: uniquely suited because, after all, this is what God has given to each one of us, his children. What is more honouring to God than that we should be like our heavenly Father as we relate to our children?

## The gift of being valued

The greatest gift anyone can ever give a child is to enable her to see that she is of infinite value and worth. Humanistic philosophy may place human beings at the centre of the universe, but the Christian faith goes one step further by saying that we are of such immeasurable value that God himself was willing to die for us so that he might have a never-ending – an eternal – friendship with us. How can we possibly understand our value in the eyes of God? We still only scratch the surface when we look at Christ on the cross: 'And Christ on the cross is more beautiful than anything –

for extreme is the cost of extremest beauty' (*Wangerin 1989, p 115*).

Surely then, for a child to learn *through* us that she is infinitely valuable to God is the greatest gift we can offer her. And *through us* is the key, for it is through us that she learns of God, learns to reach out and touch him – and, thank God, it is also despite us, for, as our heavenly Father knows, we so often fall short.

A tragic reflection on our world today is the fact that a child's sense of self-worth is destroyed in so many ways. Many of these are public: child exploitation whether through work or war or want, child sexual abuse, children forced to leave home and live on the streets. The list is endless. Such children feel totally worthless. Other ways are more subtle, even unconscious, and we fall into them ourselves. For example, ridiculing a child's comments. How easy it is to put down a child: 'What do you know about it?', 'You don't know what you're talking about'. Often we respond like this to save our own face: we are protecting our own sense of self-worth from being embarrassed or 'shown up'.

At other times, we may ignore a child's work: 'Not now, can't you see I'm busy?', 'All right, put it on the table. I'll look at it later'. This can devastate a child who has been busy putting together a somewhat messy 'creation' for hours, and happens to choose an inopportune moment to present it.

Often we prioritise adult interests: 'Come on, this is a much better book to read than that one', when she has been storing up a special book for her bedtime story. We are often guilty of denying the validity of a child's feelings: 'Don't cry, you're not a baby', 'Don't get so excited or I may not take you after all'. A response like this dampens a child's emotions and can leave her thinking that her feelings are wrong, that they are not of value.

All of these responses discount the child and her contributions. A steady diet of this results in the child's sense of self-esteem gradually being whittled away. The message received consciously or unconsciously is, 'What you have to give is really of very little value', and by extension, 'You are of very little value'. And how can the grown-up be wrong? After all, the child has to depend on the adult for everything and needs the approval offered.

When it comes to making a decision, the child ends up feeling worth very little in many areas, and lacks confidence in herself. This can lay the foundations for making her prey to all sorts of negative influences in order to scrape back some vestige of self-esteem: drugs, sex and petty crime, can all play a part at a later stage, as she struggles to find some area in which she can achieve a sense of being 'someone', of being 'of worth'.

We can play a major role within our homes and our children's groups in reversing this trend, or in preventing it from starting. If we can act as an advocate for the children, affirming their worth and value to us, and set this within the context of their worth and value to God, then we will have laid a major foundation for a mature and realistic faith as they grow older (in terms of their understanding of their own value). It is most important that we value children *in their own right*, regardless of whether they conform to the rules of the group, do well, attend regularly, or whatever. Thus, we celebrate with the children not what they achieve, but who they are.

Within our church groups, this can be done by finding out as much as possible about the child's world outside church: where he lives, family details, likes/dislikes, pets, birthdays, holidays, and so on. A sharing time is essential if each child is to feel he is valued and that what he has to say is worth listening to. Sometimes sitting a child on a special chair or cushion or giving him a particular item to hold can be a sign to the group that this particular person has 'the floor'. This may be the only time in the entire week that a child is able to feel really valued. This is a good, positive feeling. A child experiencing this will come back for more and can learn that God values him in just the same way.

During these sharing or news times, it is essential that the leader notes down what is said, to follow up with a visit in the week or a question the next time they meet. What better way of building the children's self-esteem than to make them realise that what they had to say was so important that you have taken the trouble to remember it and follow it up!

It is also important in children's groups that children can express what they are feeling and discover that it is all right, that it is safe, and that it is not discounted. It may well be important for Danny to learn that he can cry with frustration and anger at not having won a game. He needs to experience that he is not simply condemned outright, but that there is someone available to talk with him about why he feels as he does and to help him explore a different response.

A further way in which we can affirm a child's sense of self-worth is by shifting the balance in our groups away from achieving.

49

It is all too easy for the school ethos to creep in: stars for attendance, for learning the memory verse, for bringing a friend. 'It's a good incentive, it works!' you may say, pointing to the stars. But what about Jason who gets few or none? 'That's okay,' you may say. 'We don't force anyone to do things. And we know his home background and understand his problems.' And Jason may well appear not to be bothered. But as he watches the stars being given to others, what's happening to his own sense of worth? The effects of a difficult home background are, perhaps, actually being reinforced by the Sunday group.

If you feel an incentive element to be important, look for situations within the group for which stars can be given. For example, why not encourage positive behaviour: one star each time you see a child helping another? Then there is no reason why Jason shouldn't receive some stars. And it may challenge those from church-going backgrounds who always get attendance and memory verse stars, to think a little more deeply about what is being encouraged and taught in the group.

Your recognition of a child's worth can also be communicated by the way in which you organise your group and delegate tasks. How much do you involve the children in setting out or decorating the room, carrying out tasks, deciding the rules, planning the programme, welcoming newcomers, and so on. Giving children responsibility and involving them in decisions says, 'I think your ideas are of value. I believe you can do this. Therefore, you are of value.'

Clearly it is not possible, or desirable, to involve children in every aspect of the group, but in my experience there is often scope for a much higher level of involvement than we usually offer. But recognise also that it won't be easy, because in delegating a task there is always the risk that it won't happen in the way you would wish. Yet to interfere, to say, 'No, don't do it like that,' can make a child's growing sense of self-esteem plummet. The best approach is to strike a balance and tackle a task together. Then if you sense that a particular decision is not the best, look first for an opportunity to praise: 'I think those welcome cards you've made are really good', then gently suggest an alternative approach: 'How do you think you would feel if you were visiting a group for the first time? Would you like to sit at the front of the group? Do you think . . .'

In many ways a child's developing sense of self-worth is like a butterfly emerging from a chrysalis. As the sun warms the damp wings, the insect makes small attempts to stretch them out and enable them to dry and grow stronger. But a careless touch by a human can hinder the process. In the same way, we need to encourage and nurture the growth of the child's self-esteem in every way possible, being careful not to damage it by carelessness, insensitivity, or just plain ignorance. But does this sound daunting? What about the times when, for whatever reasons, we respond to a child instinctively, without thinking about the 'right' response? D W Winnicott, the paediatrician referred to above, uses the lovely phrase the 'good enough' mother. By extension, we may speak about the 'good enough' Sunday group leader or the 'good enough' children's worker. No one, our children included, expects us to be perfect. God himself knows that we are frail human beings, capable of mistakes. Our responsibility is, with God's help, to be 'good enough'. If we respond or act unthinkingly, then we apologise. Children respect adults who can admit they were in the wrong and will forgive. And through such an experience, a child's sense of self worth may even be increased as she sees that she is of enough value to warrant an apology.

## The gift of being listened to

As adults we cram so much into our days. We have work to go to, shopping to do, relations to visit, children to take here, there and everywhere, meals to cook, homes to care for, Sunday group material to prepare . . . Oh, here's Kevin, just home from Cubs and lots to tell. Of course, we'll listen to Kevin while we're mending the iron. 'What's that Kevin? Just a second while I get another screwdriver. No, that's not how the story goes . . . Jasper never did find the cave. Oh, sorry, you were told to write a different ending? Could you just pass me that screw over there?'

Sound familiar? We all do it. And often it can't be helped. But there need to be times too when children are given our full, undivided attention and are listened to properly, not just heard. Listening properly means that our whole attention is focused on the child. It may mean that we stop whatever else we have been doing, and actually sit down and engage face to face with the child. It certainly means that we maintain eye contact. As we listen, we take in, understand and reflect on what we are hearing so that our perception of the speaker and of the subject changes.

This is an activity that shows great respect for the speaker. It shows that we consider both the speaker and the subject matter to be of enough importance to warrant our full attention. Certainly, we don't necessarily absorb the subject matter uncritically. We may comment on or rephrase what is said in our own terms. This is all part of the shaping process by which a child learns, but this is based on valuing her starting point. A child who is listened to respectfully and with whom an adult interacts on an equal level is a child who develops a sense of self-respect and confidence. She is the child who grows up knowing that she has something of value to offer to others.

Have you ever thought about how hard it is for some adults to defend their faith? They are often those who, as children, were not properly listened to, or whose opinions were not sought after or valued. They have grown up without the ability to express their own beliefs confidently because when they have asserted their thoughts or ideas in the past, they have been ignored or belittled.

Listening may be for you a normal part of your everyday life. But for many children it is not – and some of these children may well be a part of your Sunday group. How can you show these children that you, at least, value their contributions? Why not provide opportunities for a child to be listened to? This may be during a sharing or news time as described above. Talking times following an activity may be another opportunity. Then how about inviting children to recap what happened during the previous session, recalling the theme, story or whatever?

In each case, think carefully about how much time you give to each child. It is very easy to listen more to the fluent child who can express herself quickly and easily, or to the child who is always ready to contribute first. But equal time needs to be given to the slow, hesitant speaker, to the child who tends to go off at a tangent or whose contribution never seems to be quite relevant. That child, too, deserves to be listened to, perhaps needs to be listened to even more than the fluent child.

In listening it is very important to allow the child time to complete her contribution. This is especially true for a child who has difficulty in expressing herself. If *you* are tempted to cut her short, knowing as you do the importance of listening, think how often this probably happens to her elsewhere. It is also important not to interrupt a child: just as we ask children not to interrupt adults, so we should accord a similar respect to children and not interrupt them.

There certainly will be occasions when, because of time constraints, we cannot allow a child to talk for too long, especially if he has gone off at a tangent. In that case, wait for a suitable opportunity to interject first a comment on the subject he has been talking about (so he knows you have actually been listening), and then an honest explanation of the situation followed by an open invitation to talk further later. Thus, 'Jack, I think it's amazing that you actually counted 37 slugs. I bet there were lots more hiding in the grass. We're going to think about how the shepherd counted his sheep now, otherwise you won't have a story to tell your mum when you get home, but I'd like to hear more about those slugs afterwards. Okay?'

*'Jack, I think it's amazing that you counted 37 slugs.'*

Above all, do *listen*, don't just hear. As you sit there listening to the slug story, it would be very easy to think, *Let's see, what have I got to do next?* 'Wow, slugs were they, Jack?' *Oh dear, how can I stop him?* *We must move on.* 'Yes, red slugs?' *This just isn't relevant* . . . Children are very sensitive to an adult who is only half-listening. Put away your agenda during your listening time and give the child your complete attention. A child who has experienced the gift of being listened to well will never forget it.

'I really enjoy going to that Sunday group. They really listen to you there. And do you know, they say that God listens to me in the same way. Isn't that something!'

## The gift of being accepted unconditionally

This is perhaps the easiest gift to give to some children and the hardest to give to others. When little James removes the poster you have put up on the board for the umpteenth time, you can't help but love him even though he's being so annoying: he's got such a winning, mischievous smile under his curly red hair. But when Robert starts bouncing yet again on the cushions stacked neatly in the corner – cushions you've already restacked twice! – you feel your principle of unconditional acceptance stretched to the limit.

Robert is not the sort of child you automatically warm to. His eyes always carry an unspoken challenge, a dare which seems to say, 'I'm going to see just how far I can push you'. He keeps you at arm's length all the time, never allowing you to get emotionally or physically close. He never appears to become involved with the group either, but is always on the periphery, never really taking in the story, but always with half an eye on what the other children are doing. When he chooses, he can be very disruptive. Yet unconsciously, Robert is saying, 'Okay, this is Sunday group. You say God loves us. You say you love all of us. Let's see if you really love me. At home they don't care what I do.'

Robert desperately needs to be loved and cared for regardless of what he says and does. He represents one of the hardest types of children to integrate into a traditional Sunday group. And it may well be at the end of the day that he has actually 'learned nothing' – at least nothing in terms of factual material from the Bible. What he may well have learned, however, which is far more important for him at this stage in his life, is that you are able to accept him just as he is, that the group atmosphere has remained welcoming and accepting of him. And once he has experienced this acceptance from you, he will begin to understand when you say that Jesus also loves him unconditionally.

But unconditional acceptance does not only need to apply to a difficult child. This type of acceptance also relates to recognising the validity of a child's feelings at a given moment without rejecting the child. What parent hasn't set a boundary for a child and encountered the response, 'I hate you'. Real, unconditional acceptance means accepting the child's feelings at that moment. We may not like to hear such words, they may hurt, but we need to do something creative with such feelings. We need to explore what lies behind the words. Perhaps it is, 'I'm really feeling angry with you for setting that boundary. It makes me feel different from my friends.' Rephrasing it in this way accepts the child, feelings and all, and encourages some useful interchange about the issue.

At another level, how many of us – parents, Sunday group leaders and others – have heard the complaint, 'I don't want to go to church. I hate church'? It is easy to judge immediately: 'You shouldn't say that. What's the matter with it?' But if we accept that the child's feelings are valid for him at that given moment, then we can follow up his comments. We may well discover that he is bored, that he perceives the service as geared to adults with only token recognition of children. *We* may not see it like that. But the point is that he does and therefore, whilst we may disagree with him, we can still accept him and his feelings. This acceptance can then provide the basis for exploring the issue further.

*But* – and this is a big 'but' – unconditional acceptance does not mean allowing the child to walk all over you. Children feel safer and grow better within clear boundaries. You owe it to the children with whom you live and work to make clear both what the boundaries are and what will happen if they are overstepped. This raises the issue of discipline and how it is handled. A very creative approach to discipline and punishment is set out in *Stress and Your Child* by Dr Archibald D Hart, who says,

> The purpose of discipline is to teach self-control and obedience to reasonable social rules. This goal is best met not through punishment (which is usually motivated by anger and a desire for revenge), but by a carefully thought-out plan of logical consequences for misbehaviour. Parents should present a united front, try to be fair, use positive reinforcement, anticipate problems, discipline promptly, aim for consistency and involve the whole family in designing the discipline plan.
>
> (*Hart 1992, p 154*)

Whilst Hart's approach is set in the context of the family, it can equally apply to children's workers in church or other settings.

Of particular interest is, first, his view that the purpose of discipline should be 'to teach self-control and obedience to reasonable social rules'. Usually, we tend to equate discipline with punishment. Here it has a much more positive connotation and places the onus for making the rules work jointly on the child and the adult.

A second important point is that the whole family – or children's group – should be involved in designing the 'discipline plan'. This means that the whole group can 'own' the plan and, when a group has been closely involved in designing such a plan, then they will be much more committed to keeping it. A third significant point is that the plan consists of a series of 'logical consequences for misbehaviour' (ie, 'What happens to you if you do that?'). In other words, it sets up a series of boundaries which – as it will be drawn up together with the children – a child can understand and choose to respect.

And if not, at least, the child knows what the consequences will be, which can take an enormous load off the shoulders of the leader. She does not need to feel that *she* is always singling out one particular child for discipline, since the group as a whole has set the boundaries. But above all, regardless of the discipline that has to be exercised, the leader can still demonstrate her unconditional acceptance of the child. For in accepting a child unconditionally, in loving him for who he is, not for what he does, she is according him value and worth because she is loving him as Jesus does. She is saying, in effect, 'I know you're not there yet (nor am I), but I love you just as you are right now.' What a gift to give a child!

With such gifts as these, modelled by Christian caregivers, a child cannot help but grow and deepen in her understanding of Jesus as friend and Saviour. If a child experiences receiving these gifts as a positive, affirming experience, and if the caregiver in turn is constantly radiating Christ and pointing towards him, then a child will want to know more about the source of these gifts.

This is why, in order to be fully effective in sharing the good news of Jesus, an ablity to enter the child's world has to be coupled with an ability to help the child see how Jesus can be a part of that world. To re-emphasise it, an ability to enter the child's world is wonderful; an ability to share the truth of the Bible is wonderful. But unless the two are combined, we will always be less than fully effective in introducing children to Jesus and in laying the foundations for a growing faith. We need to be an advocate for the child and his world, leading him to our friend, Jesus.

## Thinkabout

**1** What can you do in your home or in your children's group to ensure that each of your children feel really valued?

**2** When did you last speak with a child? Did you really listen or did your own agenda keep creeping in? What can you do to avoid this happening?

**3** If you were to set up a 'discipline plan' for your group or for your children at home, what elements would it include? How does this reflect the needs of your group/family?

# PART II

# The child as God's representative

– Thinking about Jesus' love for children –

*It is the relationship with Jesus which makes these children representatives of God. As such they are our teachers. In their objective humility and need they cry 'mother', 'father', 'Abba', and they stretch out their empty hands. If we want to learn how to become God's representatives, we must learn it from the child in our midst.* Hans Reudi-Weber

# 6. JESUS AND CHILDREN

As far as we know, the relationship that Jesus had with children while here on earth turned the contemporary Jewish approach upside down. Whilst the Jewish community did not inflict extremes of discipline or practise child exposure as did their Roman and Spartan contemporaries, neither did the child have much value except in terms of needing to be educated – if he were a boy.

It's hard to envisage, used as we are to the western world's attitude to children, how absolutely revolutionary Jesus' approach must have appeared to his followers. Why, they were only protecting his interests when they shooed the children away, but Jesus actually became angry with them. The next thing they knew, Jesus was telling them that if they were to welcome a child in his name they would, in effect, be welcoming him. This was unbelievable! In the first place, they weren't in the habit of bothering much with children. Then 'in my name' carried the implication that the child was Jesus' representative. If a king sent an envoy, that envoy was sent in the king's name. Could Jesus really be saying that a child had this kind of special relationship with him?

But the disciples had yet another surprise coming: Jesus

61

challenged them to change and *become like a child* if they wanted to enter the kingdom of heaven. In other words, Jesus was inviting them to change their whole approach to children: to see them as valuable, to see them as his representatives, to welcome them and in doing so to welcome him, and to take on their qualities, qualities of a simple faith, humility and a trusting openness. Above all, Jesus was inviting them to take on his own deep love of children.

Many of the images used in the Bible when referring to God's love for us picture the deep longing, giving, enriching and self-sacrificing love of parent for child. Through these images, we are privileged to see the quality of love God has for us, his children, and, by extension, for all children, and to feel his pain as children are unloved, abused and destroyed. One of the most moving of these passages comes in Hosea 11:4, in which God speaks of his longing love for Israel using the image of a parent with a child. Here one can picture how God would be with children and how he wants us to be:

> I drew them to me with affection and love
> I picked them up and held them to my cheek
> I bent down to them and fed them.

No tall adult here, towering above the small child, but bending down, getting on her level and nourishing her. And note the importance of touch. 'I picked them up and held them to my cheek' – surely a sign of intimate love and tenderness, since in a face we can see the soul of a person.

Then, there is a passage in Isaiah 66:12–13:

> You will be like a child that is nursed by its mother,
> carried in her arms, and treated with love.
> I will comfort you . . .
> as a mother comforts her child.

Here is a picture of the bonding between mother and child, as the child is fed at the breast, and is then carried in his mother's arms and loved as she goes about her duties. Then, when sadness comes, with it comes comfort and tenderness: the available mother, present as her child needs her. One calls to mind a picture of the mother in the two-thirds world who carries her baby in a sling at her breast while she works, ready to feed, love and comfort the child as the need arises.

# Advocates for children

It is not my intention here to review what has been written about Jesus and children. But I always find it challenging to read through the Gospels and note the specific instances where Jesus had contact with children (or young people since we do not always know their age). If these meetings have been written down, think how many others there must have been. I can picture children flocking to see Jesus as he travelled around, shy ones hanging back, brave ones getting as near to the front of the crowds as possible, all listening to and absorbing the love that flowed from him.

We read how Andrew introduced to Jesus the young boy, whose bread and fish lunch was shared with thousands (John 6:8–15). We read of the persistence of the mother on behalf of her daughter (Mark 7:24–30), the father on behalf of his son, in begging Jesus to cast out evil spirits, which Jesus did (Mark 9:14–32). We read of the government official seeking healing for his son, which Jesus gave (Mark 5:21–43).

There is one important point to note from all these accounts. In each case, the child or young person had an advocate, an adult who spoke to Jesus on their behalf. So, while on the one hand we are challenged to become *like* children, we are also set the example of becoming advocates *for* children, available to take them to see Jesus. This is not to say, of course, that a child cannot come to Jesus on his own. But if we are involved with children in some capacity, then the more we become like children ourselves, the better we will understand how to lead them to Jesus and to advocate on their behalf. This leads us to our next point.

## Jesus' messages to adults

What are Jesus' messages to us as adults regarding children? There are many, but let us note ten:

1 Jesus challenges us to be advocates for children. We are to care for them as he did, and not to stand in their way (Mark 10:14). This can mean defending their interests when they have no one else to support them. For example, you may pick up from a casual (or not so casual!) comment in your group that a child is experiencing difficulties at home. Further caring enquiries may show that the parents' relationship is very fragile and the child feels uncertain, frightened and unsupported. You can advocate for

the child, not necessarily by becoming involved in the home situation (although on occasion this might be appropriate), but by structuring the group and related activities in such a way as to help the child feel specially cared for and listened to.

You might also advocate for a child when something really good has happened to her, by providing an opportunity for celebration and praise – a good chance to boost a child's sense of worth. You can also advocate for the child by personally familiarising yourself with the many resources available in order to help you improve your understanding of, and skills in, working with children so that you keep fresh in your approach to them.

And, most importantly, you can advocate that children's interests and needs are placed high on your church's agenda. (For example, are services planned to take into account the need for children to worship together with the whole church family?) In doing this, you may sometimes find that you are not very popular, but it is vital that the important position of children is recognised. For parents or other children's workers, this may well mean arguing a point at school, or engaging with secular bodies to ensure that the needs and rights of children are recognised and respected.

On a wider front, we should all become advocates for children in other parts of the world who suffer exploitation and abuse to a degree we can scarcely imagine. Agencies such as *Tear Fund*, *Save the Children* and *Amnesty International* all supply information and methods of advocacy.

But advocacy also means prayer on behalf of children. And this is not once-in-a-while prayer. It is persistent, determined, loving prayer – prayer that comes out of a heart of love like that of God himself. It is prayer that cares passionately about each individual child. Do we advocate for our children like this before God?

2 Jesus commends children to our loving care; we are to welcome them (Mark 9:37). A welcome isn't grudging. It is arms flung wide, an open smile, taking a real pleasure in the one you are welcoming. Children need to experience that kind of welcome from us. How do we respond to children in our group when we meet them in the street? Do we give them just a casual nod, perhaps feeling awkward to know what to say to them outside the secure confines of the group and our role as leader?

Equally, how do they respond to us? Do they rush up and start chatting, or do they hang back, hoping we haven't noticed them?

Sometimes the freedom a child feels is related to how they address us. It may be hard to get away from the school model when using the 'Mr', 'Miss' or 'Mrs' title, although some prefer this. Sometimes using 'Auntie' (or 'Uncle') provides another approach, while yet others opt for the use of first names. But how many times have I been frustrated myself as, despite all my efforts, children lapse back into a school mode, raising their hands and shouting excitedly, 'Miss, Miss!' Titles are useful tools, but primarily it is the atmosphere of unreserved love and welcome which touches the child.

All too sadly, one area in which children often do not feel genuinely welcomed in church is in their reception by the adult community. This may be in the worship service where they feel guests at, rather than a part of, the worship service. It may be at social events where they feel on the periphery. They feel, often quite rightly, that the adults do not know how to relate to them and, therefore, ignore them or make them feel unwanted. This is so contrary to Jesus' teaching that a strong, stern advocacy needs to be made on behalf of the children to church leaders, to ensure that attitudes change. Otherwise children will simply stop coming to church, feeling unwelcomed and unwanted.

3 Jesus reminds us that he has a special relationship with children: we are to welcome them in his name as his representatives (Mark 9:37). This special relationship draws on the qualities of simplicity, trust and openness which Jesus prizes. Do we, like Jesus, have a special relationship with our children?

Within our groups this special relationship can be shown by remembering important days such as birthdays, and by sending cards. It can be shown by remembering what has been said at news times one week and following it up the next week. It can be shown by planning special activities to do together as a group outside church: a swimming party, a farm visit, a video evening. We need to explore ways in which to be creative in our relationship with the children, so that they can look at the quality of their relationship with us and be drawn to see beyond it to the quality of relationship they can have with Jesus. As parents, this can be modelled in the time we give to just being with, or playing with, our children: showing that they are entitled to quality time with us.

4 Jesus further reminds us that in welcoming the child we welcome him. So, too, in welcoming him we welcome God, the one

who sent Jesus. Thus, as we respond to the child, the blessings of the presence of the Son and the Father also come to us. The next time you reach out and welcome a child, remember in whose name he comes, and welcome also the Son and the Father. What a marvellous thought!

5 Jesus commands that we change and become like children in order to enter the kingdom (Matthew 18:3). We have already looked at how we might enter the child's world, how we might become like a child. We need to take time to be, time to play, time to listen, to watch and to read. We need to see what our childhood experiences have to say to us today. Above all, we need to take on the qualities of childlikeness: simple trust, openness, freely offered joy and love. We will look at these below in terms of changing and making these qualities a part of our approach to God, so that we are able to enter the kingdom.

It isn't to the wise or rich that the kingdom is offered but to those who, in human terms, are poor and simple – yet another blessing for those who become like a child. This surely is a tremendous encouragement to those of us who often feel out of our depth with theological arguments.

6 Jesus commands us not to despise children (Matthew 18:10). 'Little ones' here may refer to those who are 'little' in the faith, but the truth remains unchanged. Just because children are small, without influence, often overlooked, is no reason to look down on them or ignore them. Kingdom values do not relate to size or power. Because in worldly terms children have little or no voice, it is very easy to fall into the trap of treating them as being of secondary importance.

How do we prepare for our children's groups? Is it last minute: 'Oh, well, this will do for them. They're not fussy!'? Is it uncreative: 'I've got some colouring-in that will fill in the time.'? Is it more important to do our 'adult bit' after church when there is a lost-looking six-year-old hanging around at the door waiting for mum to collect him?

Then, what about the room where we hold our group? How does this reflect our attitude to our group? Certainly, there are often limitations or restrictions as to the possibility of decorating a room, but a real desire to make the best of a situation, coupled with creativity, can overcome big obstacles.

*How do we prepare for our children's groups? Is it last minute?*

7 Jesus gives a stern warning that causing a child to lose faith is terrible, it is better to be drowned (Matthew 18:6). Again 'little ones' may not specifically apply to children, but the truth does. Causing a child to lose faith can be done so easily, so subtly. An adult group leader can become a role model, or example, for a child. If the adult slips, the watching child, too, can follow suit.

As advocates for the child, there is a tremendous responsibility placed on us. What do we model for our children? We should be modelling Christ. A child needs to look at us and see someone whose relationship with Christ is of paramount importance, someone for whom prayer and a dependence on God's word are central. They also need to see someone who has time for them and an understanding of them. They need to see someone who will advocate for them, who will fight on their behalf. They also need to see someone who can play with them and have fun. They need to see someone who is real, who makes mistakes, who slips and falls, but who can recognise and admit mistakes, ask for forgiveness, and start again. They need to see someone in whom they can catch a glimpse of Jesus and know that he really can change lives, that he is worth following.

8 Jesus said, 'Do not stop the children coming to me' (Matthew 19:14). Here is both a joy and a responsibility. The joy is that

Jesus' arms are always open to children. As many as come, there is still room for more. The responsibility on us is that we don't stand in the way as the disciples were doing. Do we hinder by our adult attitudes and expectations as the disciples did? Often it is so hard for us to step outside our adult perspective. The disciples didn't mean to be unkind to the children; neither do we. They were trying to care for Jesus. But Jesus didn't want to be cared for like that.

Perhaps sometimes, we want to care for ourselves too much: this is my time, those are my belongings, this is my day off, this is my conversation . . . Certainly we need time for ourselves, time to be 'adult', but at other times we need to be like Jesus, to be willing to put our own feelings aside and go the second mile for our children. And we do need to ensure that our adult expectations: 'You should behave like this', 'That is not appropriate at church', 'This is something you need to learn', do not hinder the child. We need to ensure our tone of voice, our facial expressions, our attitudes do not turn a child away. How can we do this? Become like a child, Jesus said, see me as a child does, and then you will not stand in the way.

9 Jesus reminds us that God's kingdom belongs to those such as children (Matthew 19:14). 'Those such as children' are surely those who have taken on board the qualities of a child, qualities of simplicity, humility, trust and openness. Here we do not only enter the kingdom, but take possession of it: it belongs to us. 'Belonging' often has a 'this is mine' connotation, but if we have taken on board these qualities, then what we will be saying is, 'This can be yours, come and see'.

How can we share this wonderful gift with our children? How can we make the Gospel 'attractive'? Certainly for children's workers, good resource material, creative approaches to presenting biblical material, and a warm, welcoming, caring group atmosphere are fundamental. A knowledge of children and their strengths and needs is essential. But above all, we share the gift of who we are ourselves. If we have taken on those qualities that enable us to enter the kingdom, then the children should be able to see Jesus in us. When God wanted to show his redeeming love to the world, he didn't send books or programmes, he sent a living, breathing, loving, caring man. Our programmes may be the best there can be, but it is in their relationship with us that children are going to see and feel a faith that is alive.

10 Jesus reminds us that children and babies can offer perfect praise (Matthew 21:16). There is no need to wait for them to grow older, to 'mature'. This verse speaks of the child's value *now*, just as she is. This is a strong, positive affirmation of the completeness of a child's offering to God. It doesn't need maturing, it doesn't need refining, it is 'perfect praise' just as it is now. This is also a sharp warning to those of us who are tempted to tamper with or 'improve' upon a child's offering to God.

How many times, in taking a group of children into the church worship service, do we find that they are 'tolerated' rather than 'welcomed'? Perhaps as adults we need educating as to the truth of this verse. Certainly, a child's worship is not as ours would be, and we may not feel at ease with it. But it is essential that we recognise that it is every bit as valid as our expression of worship, and as such we must respect it and do our best to enter into it. And in so far as we (adults and children) are the body of Christ, we must worship together. All-age services are not an option, they are an essential demonstration of our unity as God's family, and each age-group must be given the opportunity to contribute. Each person and each offering must be recognised as being of equal importance in God's eyes.

As we work with children, as we parent children, we would do well to review these ten points periodically to see if we are following the spirit of Jesus' commendations and commandments to us regarding children.

## Thinkabout

1 Within the church structure, children do not normally have a voice. Are there ways in which you can advocate for the children within your church?

2 If you look to Jesus as a role model of how to respond to children, what should you be doing in your situation to follow his example?

3 If you *were* to follow Jesus' example, would you be willing to take the consequences of this in a setting which is primarily adult-centred?

# 7. CHILDREN AND THEIR SPIRITUALITY

## Jesus affirms the child

In the passages just explored, Jesus affirms the important place of the child. He points out that a child has a special relationship with God; that a child is a representative of God; that a child has certain qualities which we, as adults, need if we want to enter the kingdom of heaven, and that a child's expression of praise to God can be complete here and now. All of this points to the fact that Jesus recognised in children a deep spirituality and an openness to God.

Spirituality is one of those words that has come into vogue these days – indeed, it even features in the National Curriculum. It has been defined in many ways, sometimes with a specifically Christian content, sometimes with a broader definition relating simply to an openness to 'that which is other,' ie, non-material.

A child's spirituality may be defined as an innate sensitivity to matters beyond, and yet within, everyday life. However, it is important to note that children themselves are not aware that this is anything special: for them it is just part and parcel of who they are as children. Thus, it has to do with gifts of seeing, of trust, of openness to believe, of spontaneity, of curiosity, of 'unclutteredness', of simplicity – all of which are qualities that enable a greater openness to, and understanding of, God. This is unconscious faith, if you like. It is that which enables a child to marvel at anything from a seashell to a slug because God has put the urge and the ability to marvel within the child's soul.

As we get older, we lose these qualities. They become cluttered, clouded by adult concerns. We don't even see a seashell because we've no time to visit the seaside. As for slugs, well, they're just garden pests to be destroyed. Wordsworth's poem, *Ode: Intimations of Immortality from Recollections of Early Childhood*, reminds us:

> Heaven lies about us in our infancy!
> Shades of the prison-house begin to close
> Upon the growing Boy . . .

Above all, we lose the quality of simple trust, hence Jesus' injunction to us to 'become like a child'.

## The riches of the child's spirituality

Let us now look in greater detail at the qualities that enable the child to be open and receptive to God, in other words, the riches of the child's spirituality.

1 The child has a natural sensitivity to the world and to nature. This is not just a vague, 'Oh that's nice', but a profound sense of awe and wonder. He marvels at the rainbow in a spray of water, at the wind-blown lightness of a dead bee, at an ant carrying a snack twice its size, at the different shapes and textures in gravel . . . the list is endless. I recall taking a group of east London children out to Essex on a coach trip and their utter fascination at seeing a herd of cows in a large open field. What a refreshing, rich gift this is that most of us have lost – or submerged!

2 The child has an in-touchness with feelings. As adults, we often find the expression of emotions embarrassing or threatening. A child knows them, recognises them and, if allowed, expresses them. Sometimes we may feel the time and the manner in which they are expressed to be inappropriate – especially if it is a tantrum at the church door! But at another time, this same child may well have the ability to really 'feel' the presence of God in the world around her or in a loving relationship. Sister Macrina Wiederkehr

recalls this childhood ability to 'feel' God in her book *A Tree Full of Angels*:

> The spirituality of my childhood is the one I would most like to have restored. It was pure and fresh and honest. I read God everywhere! . . . I have become too complicated in my prayer. Yet under the eye of God all shall be restored.
>
> *(Wiederkehr 1990, p 62)*

3 The child can find belief easy and uncomplicated, like the child who said quite matter-of-factly, 'I saw an angel looking in my window this morning'. As adults, we find it so hard to simply believe. We have lost the ability to make the leap of faith and to accept. Is this because we have been squeezed into the world's mould that says, 'simple = childish, complicated = maturity'?

A beautiful illustration of a child's simple faith, yet deep understanding, comes in Walter Wangerin's *The Manger is Empty* where he speaks of his seven-year-old daughter.

> 'Dad?' said Mary, who could ponder so much in her heart. 'Why are you crying?. . .'
>
> 'Because I have nothing else to say,' I said to her. 'I haven't had the words for some time now.'
>
> 'Dad?'
>
> 'What?'
>
> 'Don't cry. I can talk for both of us.'

> It always was; it always will be; it was in the fullness of time when the Christ child first was born; it was in 1981 when my daughter taught me the times and the crossing of times on Christmas Eve; it is in every celebration of Christ's own crossing; and it shall be forever – that this is the power of a wise love wisely expressed: to transfigure the heart, suddenly, forever.
>
> *(Wangerin 1989, p 19–20)*

4 The child can accept things at face value. We adults demand explanations, reasons; a child hears, receives and accepts: 'Why shouldn't Jesus have been able to walk on water? After all he *was* God'. We end up wanting to understand how it could be physically possible and losing the awe, wonder and acceptance that a child brings to the story. A child also has the ability to take as much as she needs for herself at a given time. The 'ought' or 'should' which we adults bring to our Christian experience is not there for

a child. When she has taken in enough, she will go off and play, or, if that is not possible, simply switch off.

**5** The child has an open, welcoming nature. Sadly, this has been exploited far too often in some cases, and fear creeps in. We ourselves, as children's workers, need to be 'wise as serpents and harmless as doves', alert to the possibilities of misinterpretation there might be in our dealings with children. Nevertheless, the potential openness to respond to a genuine relationship is there. This provides a wonderful opportunity for us as children's workers to introduce the child to the best friend of all – Jesus Christ.

**6** The child has a trust. If she is brought up in a trustworthy environment, so she will learn to trust, and, by extension, to understand what trust in God means. As adults, we have frequently had our trust abused. Many of us find it hard to trust, even hard to trust God. But we need to model trust. For the children, we need to be trustworthy. If we let them down, then they will find it hard to trust. This will be even more true for the child who comes from a home with very little love and constant criticism. Being trustworthy has to do with dependability, with keeping one's word, with always being there, with a willingness to forgive. Through us, children can learn what a trustworthy God is like.

**7** The child has a gift for seeing and perceiving which can make us adults uncomfortable. We may think that a child will not recall a forgotten promise. We may think that she will not notice that our preparation has been incomplete. But a child can detect insincerity in an adult a mile away, can remind us bluntly of our forgotten promise, and can cut through our attempts at leading the group with a disarming frankness that brings us back to reality. On the plus side, a child can also perceive when we are tired or under strain, and the hastily drawn picture: 'I did it for you', or the bunch of daisies can speak worlds.

A child also has a refreshing down-to-earth honesty. In the following example, Rebecca shows that she does not always find belief easy, something that adults are often embarrassed to admit.

> **Tom:** I wish I was dead.
> **Rebecca:** I do, too, sometimes. Then I could see God. Down here I don't know whether to believe in him or not.
> **Tom:** I just wish I was dead so I don't get into trouble anymore.

**8** The child has simple, basic needs. These can be physical needs: food, clothing, shelter; but also emotional: the need to be loved, to depend, to trust. A deep friendship, a nurturing community, a supportive group, can go a long way to meeting these emotional needs. The value of dependable, caring Sunday group leaders or children's workers cannot be overstressed, either in supporting a child whose emotional needs are not being met, or in reinforcing an already emotionally stable home background.

Many grown-ups can recall a single adult figure from their childhood who significantly influenced their growth as an individual and, more importantly, their growth in faith. When such a relationship is further strengthened by a caring group and a nurturing church family, the long-term effect on a child can be immense.

**9** The child has the ability to 'be', to be very *present*. Her world is the here and now world, the 'what I am feeling, doing and being now' world, and that is all-important. Relationships are most meaningful when they address this. The way in which we present biblical material is very important in this context. The child needs to see how what happened 'back then' can be applied to the 'here and now'. Likewise, she needs to see that a relationship with Jesus has meaning for 'my world', 'my friends', 'right now'. Even last week, or the day before yesterday, are forgotten. 'Today is my moment, and now is my hour. I laugh and I cry and I sing', as the song goes.

**10** Related to the previous point, the child can quickly forget the fact that she was annoyed with you over something half an hour ago. The incident in which she felt unfairly treated is finished. As adults, we remember, we mull over and we find it hard to forgive and forget. Offering and accepting forgiveness comes easily to a child. It reminds us of God's readiness to forgive us.

## Trampling on the riches

Now I can just hear some of you, having read the last section, sitting back and saying to me, 'You must live in cloud cuckoo land. If just one of my kids was like this, I'd be laughing!' Do you think I've gone over the top in attributing these qualities to children? Not so. I certainly do not operate under any misapprehension that all of our children exhibit all of these qualities all of the time. Like us adults, children are flawed individuals. They also have the potential to be hurtful, thoughtless, and mean. But that does not cancel out the riches: I believe that within every child each of these riches exists in potential, ready to be drawn out and nurtured. I am sure that if we look hard enough we can find the seeds of one of these riches in even the most difficult and frustrating of children. We may be fallen human beings, but we are nevertheless made in the image of God.

But the sad fact is that even by the age of five many of these riches have become cluttered or even deadened – all but lost. This can happen in so many ways, and to some degree it is inevitable that it will happen because we live in a sad, broken world, and each of us as a caregiver is also flawed despite our best efforts.

In particular, this 'trampling on the riches' can happen through an abusive relationship, and this does not necessarily mean physical or sexual abuse. Emotional abuse is far more widespread and very powerful because it often occurs unawares. There is the child brought up on a soulless housing estate, where a sense of awe and wonder at God's created world has very little chance to exist, let alone grow. There is the child who is not allowed to express her feelings, 'Now, now, you mustn't cry'; 'Calm down, dear, don't get angry'; 'Sit and do something quietly will you, there's no need to get so excited'.

There is the child whose world of imagination, whose fantasy world, is not taken seriously, whose flights of fancy are demeaned to be 'just a childish game'. There is the child whose trust is abused, 'Yes, I know I said I'd take you today, but I'm sorry, my plans have changed'. There is the child who perceives one thing and who is told something else. Because the adult is the authority figure, she therefore distrusts herself and her judgement, and her sense of self-worth suffers.

There is the child whose experience of having her basic needs met is unreliable, who finds that she cannot depend on people, and worse, who internalises this, believing therefore, that she is not worth caring about. There is the child whose personal world and personal space are not respected by adults: adults enter her room without knocking; drawings, 'makings', old toys are thrown away without consulting her. There is the child who experiences lack of forgiveness: a distant act of naughtiness is brought up again and again, and held as a threat over her.

The sad truth is that if even one or two of these riches are trampled on or ignored, the path to a rich, deep faith for the child is made more difficult. If he has learned that adults are at best intermittently dependable, might not God be the same? If he has experienced an old misdemeanour being resurrected, might not God actually still be secretly punishing him for something done in the past? At another level, if a child has experienced a busy Christian household where both parents are constantly 'on the go' with church activities, she may well feel that her parents care more about the church than they do about her, and she may end up feeling bitter towards God as a result, yet also guilty for feeling bitter.

Clearly, the environment in which children are brought up also has a profound influence on their ability to respond to Jesus Christ as friend and Saviour. What a child from a non-Christian home 'knows' about God will be different to what a child from a Christian family knows and the barriers to be overcome may be greater. For example, the following observation was made by a child from a non-Christian background at a church school:

**Child:** Miss, this song's got swearing in it.
**Teacher:** I don't think it can have. Which bit do you mean?
**Child:** Where it says 'Jesus Christ!'

*'Miss, this song's got swearing in it . . . where it says "Jesus Christ!" '*

Yet underneath all the layers, all the clutter, is still the basis of the child's spirituality. Perhaps some elements are more clouded than others because of the child's experiences, but nevertheless there is still a wealth of spiritual riches on which to build. And while it is not my intention here to explore the topic, I would maintain that an appeal to these God-given spiritual qualities may well help a child who has experienced severe abuse and who is emotionally lost to find her way back to wholeness much more quickly than might otherwise be possible.

## Responding to a child's spirituality

How, then, as Christian children's workers and caregivers, do we respond to the child's spirituality? There are three possible ways:

1 We can deny its existence altogether and continue with our work of teaching the Christian faith as though the child were an empty pot which needed filling. With this approach, we would see the most important aspect of working with the children to be that of instilling knowledge of Christian truths and biblical content into them, with little regard for their social or emotional needs. We would feel we had failed if they did not remember the previous week's story, or had not learned the memory verse. 'Success' would be measured cognitively by how well the children did on a quiz. 'Education' in terms of a traditional school model would predominate here.

2 We can recognise that such characteristics exist but assert that they are nothing more than the natural stages of child development, that there is nothing particularly 'spiritual' about them and that, therefore, they have no real significance in terms of benefitting the way we work with children. This approach would deny that there is anything of value to be gained from integrating secular insights in child psychology and child development into Christian work with children.

In effect, this is saying that the marvellously creative way in which God has made children and ordained that they should develop bears no relation to what we do with them in terms of Christian faith. Because the discipline of developmental psychology is based on secular research, we should not, therefore, draw on its findings. Such insights have little, if anything, to offer to a Christian approach to working with children, indeed they may be rather suspect. We must not mix biblical truth with secular insights.

3 We can recognise that these characteristics exist, that they have a spiritual dimension, and that they can provide a wonderful foundation – a God-given foundation – from which a child can begin her journey of conscious (as opposed to unconscious) faith. We recognise that it is our responsibility to tend and care for these childlike qualities, to protect them and to bring them to fruition.

We recognise that we can freely and confidently draw on the insights of child psychology and child development, provided our approach to such insights is under the guidance of the Holy Spirit and under biblical authority. We also recognise that a solid, foundational understanding of biblical content is essential if we are to help the child make the transition from unconscious to conscious faith. Finally, we recognise that our privilege is to walk with the child on this journey of faith, respecting her chosen pace, not rushing ahead nor lagging behind. We recognise that we can learn from and with the child, that we can share with her our own experience of faith, and that we can help her to make her friendship with Jesus a part of her everyday life. This is true nurture.

My experience is that the most effective, personally enriching and exciting way to help children to a lasting faith is to follow the third option. This approach enables a child's faith to be fully integrated into every part of her life. Surely this is what Jesus had in mind when he drew the following response from the lawyer: 'Love the Lord with all your heart, with all your soul, with all your strength, and with all your mind' (Luke 10:27). There is a sense of wholeness here: love the Lord with spirit, body and mind. Just as no part of our lives should remain untouched by our faith, so every facet of our lives can, under the lordship of Christ, be drawn on to bring us to faith.

So, for example, having discovered that a six-year-old's world is rooted in the here and now, let us think how we can capitalise on that quality, by acknowledging it, say, in the way we present the Bible story, and as a result, telling the story in a way which is more meaningful for her and thus will better help her apply it.

If we are challenged to enter the world of the child by our response to the wonder of the child (Part I), if we are further challenged by Jesus to become like a child, and if we accept that a child has an innate spirituality (Part II), how does this affect our relationships with children and how we work with them in a church context? That is the topic for our next section. But first, just one cautionary illustration in case we are tempted to put children on too high a plane.

**Teacher:** Who is the Helper in the song, 'Jesus send me the Helper'?
**Child:** Err – the Easter bunny?

## Thinkabout

**1** As you have grown as an adult, what elements of your childhood spirituality have been lost? Which ones would you most like to recapture?

**2** What are practical ways in which you can affirm and nurture your children's spirituality?

**3** In what ways do you or your church stifle children's spirituality?

# PART III

# Entering with the child

– Thinking about ways to help children grow in
their understanding of God –

*I now realise that only when I can enter with the children into their joy will I be able also to enter with them into their poverty and pain. God obviously wants me to walk into the world of suffering with a little child on each hand.* Henri Nouwen

# 8
## RELATIONSHIPS

As Christian caregivers and children's workers, our prayer and our task is to enable the child's spirituality and gifts to blossom into a life-long friendship with Jesus. How then do we nurture these?

There is nothing in the world that is more valuable for a child than the experience of a good relationship. Think back to your own childhood. Can you remember a special teacher, Sunday group leader, adult friend who modelled for you the qualities of a good friendship? I can.

I returned from Japan to England at the age of eight. A missionary child, I had been taught by my parents while living in a rural area of Japan. I started school in England in the middle of a term, plunged into a strange country among strange children who looked like me in terms of ethnic origin, but who were worlds apart. I was dragged screaming and crying into class in the middle of the school day by my new head teacher, who left my distraught mother at the school gate. (Parents were *not* allowed to interfere at school in those days!) My rescuer was a wonderful teacher who entered my world, rescued me from the staring eyes, befriended me and over the days and weeks that followed made life liveable again – a friendship that continued in ensuing years, even after we had gone abroad again. This is the type of relationship a child needs with us.

Let's think about four possible aspects of a good relationship with a child.

1 As we enter the world of the child, we must *respect* it and *value* it, and walk through it *with* the child. When you are taken on a guided tour of a stately home, you don't hurry on ahead of the guide, touching this and that, interrupting, arguing. As you come to know a child, you respect her world, marvelling at its depth and breadth, gradually being introduced to more of its delights. You walk with her going at her pace, the pace at which she is comfortable. You don't rush ahead prying into corners uninvited. This can often put back or even break a relationship. Sometimes you may want to hang behind, to understand something more clearly, or just to enjoy a new perspective. A child will respect you for that, but she will also clearly let you know when she wants you to get a move on. Many adults never take the time to enter the child's world: beginning where the child is at is the first step to a lasting friendship.

2 As we enter the child's world so we *grow* together with the child. It is not all taking from the child, the child doesn't have all the answers. We help shape the child's world as we share truths and experiences from our world. But we *share*, we don't preach, we don't belittle. We suggest alternative ways of looking at things. The richness of a relationship comes in the interchange between the two individuals: each grows through the influence of the other.

3 Building up a relationship with a child takes *time*. We live in a microwave age, we live in a one week mission age, we live in a 'come, tell, respond, move on' age. Meaningful relationships are not formed in this way. Trust takes a long time to build up, especially if it has been abused. Unless we are willing to give time to a relationship, we may as well not bother.

4 A relationship has to be *worked* at. Time on its own accomplishes little. We explore how to enter a child's world, we find out what it means to become like a child. Then we try to put it into practice. We make mistakes, we come away. We spend time mulling over and praying about what went wrong. We go back and try again. We work out the best way of sharing a truth or an experience. We try something completely new. We learn what it

means to love as Jesus loved. Yes, meaningful relationships have to be worked at. Numbers are not important: ten shallow relationships will have far less impact than one deep one – in fact they can sometimes simply be a waste of time. And within this one deep relationship comes the task of nurturing the child's spirituality.

## Thinkabout

**1** How do you go about building relationships with children?

**2** How much quality time do you spend engaging with children?

**3** In what ways have you grown recently through interchange with a child? What has the child taught you?

# 9. NURTURING SPIRITUALITY

## Windows of faith

When we speak of nurturing spirituality, we are essentially speaking of the means by which we build on the child's innate spirituality, or unconscious faith, and move her to a position of conscious faith. In other words, it is the process by which a child moves from understanding what it is to trust, to understanding what it is to trust Jesus. It is moving from understanding that the group leader will listen, forgive and accept, to understanding that Jesus will do the same. What is involved in this process? We need to have a clear idea of how to nurture the child's understanding because, if we can get the process more or less right, it will help the child make the link a lot more easily.

Before we go any further, however, it is important to recognise that this is only a part of the overall process of the child moving from an unconscious to a conscious faith. In the following pages, I am looking at nurture in the context of the church. However, there is a big world outside the church and each child is shaped by her family, her school, her environment and her culture. Such factors can either contribute to or detract from the nurturing process. But either way, they cannot and should not be ignored, because they are part of the world that makes the child and, more importantly, they are the world which the child has to go back to and live within. She must be able to relate her faith to her world.

But back to nurture in the church. I have found a useful starting point to be James Fowler's image of the windows of faith (see Fowler in *How Faith Grows* 1991, p 8ff). James Fowler, a leading researcher into the area of faith development, has identified seven different elements which are involved in the process of faith. These are: thinking ('How do I think about my world?'), perspective-taking ('From what viewpoint do I look at my world?'), moral judging ('How do I understand right and wrong?'), social awareness ('How does my wider world fit in?'), relationship to authority ('How do I relate to grown-ups?'), world view ('How do I see my world?') and use of symbols ('How is my spiritual side touched?'). We'll look at these in greater detail in a moment. But note that here Fowler is not speaking of the *content* of faith. We would all accept that the content of a child's faith will change as the child develops cognitively – as his understanding grows. Thus, to speak of the 'hand of God' to a child will conjure up the image of a hand (does God cut his finger nails?), whereas an adult will have developed a far more abstract understanding of this phrase.

No, what Fowler means by his use of 'windows' is 'how we do' faith, or the change in the form of our faith. Have you ever visited a marine life centre which features a walk-through glass tunnel? Through it you can view sharks, sting rays and the whole underwater world from a variety of different aspects. Then you can walk around the pool and look in through yet more windows. Finally, you can go up above and peer down into the pool. Fowler's windows of faith are somewhat like this: each window looks at the 'pool' from a different aspect, yet the 'pool' itself (the content of faith) remains the same.

For a child to grow in faith, the truths we want to communicate need to be set within the child's world and expressed at the child's level. Sometimes we will invite a child to look at the 'pool' through window 1, another time it might be window 4. Yet another time, it might be windows 2 and 5 together. But however we decide to communicate these truths, our task as Christian children's workers and caregivers is to journey with the child as she grows in her faith and invite her to look through all the different windows there are to look through. And we can best do this by following Jesus' injunction to become like children ourselves and see with childlike eyes.

Stand with a child at one of the windows in a marine life centre:

'Ooh, look at that shark's teeth!'

'Can you see that eel? Look, its head's just coming out of that pipe!'

'Wow, what beautiful fins that sting ray's got: they're so ripply!'

Stand with the child at the windows of faith:

'Look! Isn't it wonderful how Jesus can walk on the water! He must be really something!'

'You want me to be Joseph? I wouldn't want to forgive my brothers if they did that to me.'

'Is that what salt is used for? Now I understand what Jesus meant.'

In case all this sounds too abstract, let us look at a concrete example. Imagine that the Bible story for our Sunday group is the birth of Isaac, coming after God's promise of a son to Abraham. We want our group to learn that we have a God who keeps his promises. We want to build on their own experiences of people who are dependable and trustworthy to see that God can be trusted. We are certainly not expecting each child to grasp this truth with the same understanding, in the same way or at the same speed. But if we consider how we can introduce this truth to the children by using some of Fowler's seven windows, then we stand a better chance of achieving our goal. In other words, these windows show seven different approaches to nurturing a child's spirituality.

So, you first consider how a child thinks about her world: this will affect how you present the story. How does she see her world? From what perspective? Debbie has been going through a difficult time lately. What about some drama in which she can take a part? That will help build up her sense of self-esteem. And let's include some games to emphasise the theme: 'Count the stars' is ideal as no one will be 'out'. And what activities can be included to encourage a link back into the family? This is especially important for Tom whose Dad has just been made redundant. Let's think, too, about how the children see God relating to their world . . . we'll bring out the theme of God being trustworthy through the prayer-time. Let's do a visual prayer, because the children really remember well when they can see and touch . . .

And so it goes on, looking through different windows, experimenting with how best to link together the theme, the Bible story, the needs of the group as a whole, the needs of individual children, the resources available, and the world of the child. This use of 'windows' allows for each session to be creative in its approach, effective in its presentation of biblical material, and directly geared to the specific needs of the group. Now let's look in detail at these seven windows.

## Looking through the windows

### How do I think about my world? (Thinking)

We have already noted that five to seven-year-olds think in concrete, 'here and now' terms. Therefore, the way we present the sessions must reflect that. Start with the here and now of where the children are at when they arrive at their Sunday (or week day) group. They need a time of transition from their world to the group world. A sharing time meets this need and allows time for each individual child to be listened to properly. In some groups, a special chair, a microphone, or sitting behind a television 'screen' can help other children to listen better and to await their turn more patiently as they can see that they, too, will shortly be the focus of attention.

A bridge-building activity can also help the transition between where the children have come from and what they are coming into. This needs to be firmly related to their world, something to which a child from a churched or non-churched family can equally relate. But be careful: while wanting to show that coming to God's house, coming to church, is something different and special, don't make it so 'other' that the child feels ill at ease or nervous. Children of this age do not naturally compartmentalise their worlds as we adults do. Life is much more a wholeness for them: day flows into night flows into day, play into school into home into meals. Only as a child grows older does the school and the peer group assume a life of its own and a sense of separateness come in. You can see this beginning to happen in the momentary adjustment that takes place when you collect a child of this age from school and he's not quite sure whether he is happy or perplexed at seeing you.

The way in which the story is presented provides another challenge to keep in touch with the child's concrete world. Will

*The custom of anointing with oil appears most peculiar.*

the story as it stands make sense to the child's experience and world? Are explanations needed? For example, to a child in England in the 1990s, the customs of foot washing, anointing with oil, and so on, appear most peculiar. Unless their significance is explained, the story may just be filed away by the child as another oddity to be put beside that fairy story that didn't make sense. We need to earth biblical stories in the culture of the day, so that they are seen to have a context. Children need to realise that they actually did take place at a certain time in a certain country. Jesus needs to become flesh and blood for the five to seven-year-old, not an abstract spirit.

We also need to recognise that certain Bible stories are not appropriate for our age group. The story of Abraham being asked to offer up Isaac, for example, is sometimes included in children's teaching material, possibly because in it Isaac was a child. The unswerving obedient faith of Abraham is stressed, but it is the image of a father being willing to sacrifice his son which will be etched on a child's memory. And, acknowledged or not, will be the question, 'Supposing God asks my dad to do that?' or perhaps, 'How awful God must be if he asks someone to do that'.

Which raises another issue: children of this age think visually. Their world is full of images, of pictures. This does not mean that they are unable to think abstractly, but even their abstract thoughts are couched in concrete terms, as we noted before. Therefore, the best way to communicate a story or a truth to children is visually – and not just visually, but through the use of all the senses. The senses are a key to entering the child's world which we use all too little.

Are you telling the story of the loaves and the fishes? Then pass around some fish and some bread: smell and taste. Is it the story of the storm at sea? Let some children stand on the rocking boat, while others storm, wind and rain around them. Is Mary walking in the garden at the break of the day? Listen to the birds (on tape perhaps), or, if possible, walk outside feeling the freshness of the morning, looking at the new growth. Is Nehemiah trying to build the wall? Cardboard boxes will do. Let's knock it down with these bean bags. How does it feel to have your enemies destroying your wall, insulting you, and spreading lies about you?

So as we share the Bible stories with the children, they need to come alive, to be a part of the here and now for the child and thus hold the child's attention. And in a wonderful way they will freshly come alive for us as well.

The language we use presents us with another challenge to get inside the child's world. Many Sunday group leaders and children's workers tend to use a lot of abstract words and a lot of 'Christian jargon' – a shorthand, if you like, to expressing our faith. But abstract terms are unintelligible to most five to seven-year-olds. Christian jargon may well have been heard before (especially in church-going families) but, as it is rarely accompanied by an explanation, it may as well be meaningless. Listen carefully to the level of language skills and to the style of language used by your group. A challenge to us as leaders is to find phrases which can express an abstract concept in concrete language. 'Invite Jesus into your heart' can be 'Ask Jesus to be your special friend'. 'In Jesus' name' can be 'Through the power of Jesus'. Someone who is 'faithful' can be someone who 'never lets you down' or someone who 'always keeps his promises'.

Before you select a song, read through the words from the perspective of a five to seven-year-old. Can they be understood? Do they make sense? Are they true? A favourite song of my music group is 'I'm inright, outright, upright, downright, happy all the time'. I know it's because they like the actions, but are the words really true? What sense will a child make of it if she actually stops to think about the words? And this is what we want to encourage them to do. A song or a line from a song will often remain in a child's mind long after a story has gone, even on into adolescence. In fact, a song I learned as a child haunted me for years:

> 'What you are speaks so loud, that the world can't hear what you say,
> They're looking at your walk, not listening to your talk,
> They're judging by your actions everyday.'

I can't remember anymore but I used to imagine that people were watching every step I took, and because the word 'judge' had negative overtones for me, I imagined people were waiting to pounce on me critically the moment I took a wrong step. This was probably not the effect intended (I hope not anyway!) but it indicates how very careful we need to be in our selection of songs.

When teaching a new song, go through the phrases one by one with your group, making sure that they understand them. If there are one or two difficult words explain these in everyday terms making sure that no child has misheard or misinterpreted a word. Above all, check that the song makes sense to the children. Check that they enjoy singing it and find out why. A song may have excellent words from our adult viewpoint, but unless it is also fun to sing it won't be chosen or remembered. And just a note of caution when it comes to action songs: make sure the words are thought about and grasped before adding the actions. Actions are an excellent 'aide de memoir' but can take over to the exclusion of the words.

Many children (and many adults) have come away from church activities thinking that church – and therefore God – is boring. Often, in the case of children, this is because leaders have not taken into account the short attention span of children. Children today are used to short sharp bursts of information. *Sesame Street*, a favourite early years programme, presents a rapid series of different scenarios, some lasting a few seconds, some several minutes. The child's attention is kept and held and themes return again and again.

While I'm not suggesting quite such short inputs, we do need to bear in mind that children today are not accustomed to long talks. They are used to visual aids, movement, involvement, inter-action and variety. Do we reflect this in our children's groups? More importantly, do we reflect this in our Sunday worship services? Is our service truly all-age, meeting the needs of the whole family, recognising that not everyone will feel comfortable with every approach, but realising the need for give and take?

## From what viewpoint do I look at my world? (Perspective-taking)

The world of the five to seven-year-old is largely, though not entirely, egocentric. It is not impossible for her to adopt another person's viewpoint, but we need to remember that this is a growing skill. In fact, it is something we can model ourselves and encourage within the group, for example during sharing time as described above. At such times, we need to emphasise that it is the person on the 'hot spot' who has the floor. The leader, as much as the children, has no right to interrupt, and each child needs to learn to show respect for the speaker, just as she will want to be listened to when it is her turn. Setting out the boundaries of the sharing time before it begins is an important way of helping children to think of others first and will help them to become more sensitive to others.

Another related aspect is that of helping the children to take turns. This is a skill which children will acquire more quickly if they can see that you, as leader, are always fair and that each child does, in fact, get a turn. And again, as with all these approaches to effective work with children, if the child sees that you are fair and just in your decisions, they will better understand it when you speak of our heavenly Father as being fair and loving each child equally. Which leads to a related point.

Do *we*, in fact, love all the children equally? This is not always as easy to do as it may seem. But one essential is that we treat the children equally, avoiding the temptation to always choose the same children to do certain tasks. We need the ability to see the world from the child's viewpoint in order to get inside how it 'feels' for the child when her 'centre of the world' position is challenged. Thus, how *do* we choose children to do certain tasks, such as holding up a picture or taking a message? Do we understand how it 'feels' to be passed over (however valid the reasons) and are we able to acknowledge the feeling openly to the child? 'Jane, I understand that you wanted to collect those books for me but Darren was already out there. I have written your name down so I will choose you to do it next time.'

Likewise, it is important that even if you doubt Anne's ability to carry out a task, you still choose one to give her. Your belief in her, demonstrated in this way, will do a great deal for her sense of self-worth. She may well never get chosen elsewhere. And she will put extra effort into achieving her task. Don't forget to praise her as a result. It is important to remember that you can never praise children too much. Children thrive on praise like flowers do on rain. Most children get plenty of criticism and telling off at school or at home. By contrast, surround your group with an atmosphere of love and approval, not neglecting the need for reminding the group of the discipline plan if necessary, but doing so sensitively.

Which brings me to another point. As already noted, the five to seven age is the age of transition. It is not possible for a child to respond consistently all the time. Some days you will breathe a sigh of relief and think, 'Hayley is really growing up'; other days you will be tearing your hair out. Try to look at the world from the perspective of the child. Hayley may be mucking around like a three-year-old today (for whatever reason: tiredness, friction at home, worried about school . . .). You find it is no use saying, 'Stop it, come and settle down'. She doesn't need reminding of the group rules. She is just being a three-year-old in a group of five to seven-year-olds! What you need to do is respond to Hayley at the age she is at, ie, respond to her as a three-year-old. Suggest she comes and sits on your knee, provide her with an activity to enjoy off to one side. (The other children will usually tolerate a loner doing her own thing if they feel you are keeping the main session exciting!) Perhaps you need to adapt your pro-gramme to include a game a three-year-old would enjoy. Maybe Hayley needs to be the centre of attention for a few moments, so that her world still feels safe for her. Realising how a child views her world and respecting that rather than denying it, again builds up a child's sense of her own value.

Another area in which the five to seven-year-old often feels her world fall apart is when it comes to competitive games. Team games are not so hurtful, but when it comes to individual children being out, it does immeasurable hurt to a child's sense of self-worth, especially when she is called out in front of her friends. Certainly a child will experience this at school, but as Christians we should be modelling a different approach, the one that says, 'You are all important'.

Think creatively about the games you use with your group. Some games may simply be for fun, in which case try to use cooperative games, games where no one is out, where the whole fun of the game is that everyone can join in. Such a game might be 'car wash' where children take turns in being a car driving through the car wash, while the rest of the group (gently!) wash the wheels, the doors, the windows and so on. Another game might be 'Sing-a-name' where each child sings out her name around the circle. Next time around could be 'Growl-a-name', then 'Bang-a-name', passing around a percussion instrument. Name games (and name songs) are usually very popular and, again, can help a child affirm her worth – her 'me-ness' – and, by extension, her value in God's eyes. But as with all games, be sensitive to the child who may be shy, or may not want to join in, or may be having an 'off' day, and do not insist she participates.

Also important to include are those games which have a specific point to make relative to the week's theme. Here again, it is important that children are not made to feel 'out', otherwise it is very likely that the point of the story will be lost in the feelings engendered by the game. And don't forget that as the child views the world from her egocentric position, so she feels her own emotions very powerfully. Being 'out' in a game, being 'told off', feeling hurt by another child's comments, can leave her angry or in floods of tears and can throw the remainder of the session into chaos, unless you have a helper who can care for the child.

To a certain extent, the need for involvement of the whole group also applies when planning a dramatic presentation of a story. It is not always possible to give a part to each child, but try to arrange it so that those without a specific part are 'the crowd' or 'the servants' or 'the army' or whatever it might be. Again, this helps each child to feel valued and also to feel a part of the session, actively involved, not just a passive observer.

## How do I understand right and wrong? (Moral judging)
Looking through this window, two particular areas come into focus. One is in the choice of Bible stories to use with this age group. We need to be careful not to choose stories the morality of which is too advanced for children. For example, the parable of the two workers who both get the same pay at the end of the day for working different hours will seem most unfair to the children and the truth of the story will be beyond them (Matthew 20:1–16). Likewise, the story of Jesus cursing the fig tree seems on the face of it to be rather unkind to the poor old tree (Mark 11:12–14).

In the Old Testament, many stories in the history of the Israelite people are far too cruel and violent to be suitable for using with our age group and can appear wrong in the light of the teaching 'You must not kill'.

Sometimes it is possible, however, to teach the underlying principle, allowing details to be filled in as the child grows older and a greater understanding develops. For example, 'do not commit murder' is unlikely to be an issue for our age group, but we can still teach the positive aspect: the sanctity of life, looking, for example, at how we are to care for others (Luke 10:25–37). 'Do not commit adultery' is also a difficult subject – in many ways! But we can still teach a respect for relationships, for family life as appropriate to our own group, recognising the importance for family groupings to spend time together. We can focus on the elements that go to make up the sort of family life that God wants (Deuteronomy 6:1–9).

The second area to come into focus when looking through this window is that of how issues of right and wrong, of discipline are handled within the group. We noted above, when talking of unconditional acceptance, the value of having established a discipline plan – a set of rules – with the group. This does not need to, and indeed should not, have 'heavy' rules, but simple guidelines designed to help the group operate in the best interests of every group member.

It will depend on the nature of your group as to what sort of 'guidelines' you draw up. Some groups may need guidelines to do with respect for each other, others to do with respect for property or resources, still others to do with levels of noise or movement. Whatever boundaries you choose to set, ensure that you decide on them together with your group and that you decide on a suitable response for infringement. As you draw up such guidelines together, and as they are reviewed or enforced within the group, use each occasion as an opportunity to talk about right and wrong, fair and unfair, about forgiveness, about deciding to waive the consequence (mercy), about how God views such matters.

Another area to be aware of is that children of our age group are just getting to the point of developing a strong sense of justice – or fairness. We encounter comments like, 'But Catherine only did it last week and I haven't had a turn for ages'; 'It's not fair, how come Alan gets to sing with both age groups and I don't?' These are not always easy to handle, especially when we know

we've chosen Catherine again because she did it well, and Alan because he sings in tune and the questioner doesn't! In some cases, we may need to give a direct account for our choice, pointing out how the challenger can be involved in another area. But above all, we always need to be seen as fair in our course of action, always showing, by our example, a respect for each child.

### How does my wider world fit in? (Social awareness)

The typical five-year-old is just beginning to move away from the family into the wider world. As school features increasingly large in her expanding world, so her perspective changes. School friends become important, after-school activities involve her, school enters the home through spelling, home-reading schemes and requests for parental help. But still the five-year-old's central focus will be her family. The seven-year-old has already made the transition to the outside world, but even she comes back at the end of the day to the security of home and family.

As we relate to this age group, we must realise that, for lasting impact, we need to work with the child's family. We cannot build up an effective long-term relationship by working in isolation. Certainly, it is possible for a young child to make a conscious decision to continue coming to church and to maintain a real friendship with Jesus without any support from his family, but this is the exception rather than the rule. Families can withdraw a child, families can pick up and move, families can become antagonistic, and our contact with the children is lost.

Keeping channels of communication with caregivers not just open, but alive, should be a primary task for leaders of this age group. This is for several reasons:

1 With reference to unchurched families, it helps to take away the 'mystique' of what church is and make it understandable and accessible. When we are regular church-goers ourselves, it is easy to lose sight of how very 'foreign' the church is to non-church-goers. Strange practices take place within the church (you never know whether to stand, sit or kneel), strange songs are sung (where else do adults sing except at football matches!), and obscure words are often spoken.

In some areas, the strangeness associated with church is compounded by having a stigma attached to those who attend: it is a sign of weakness, a habit only suitable for women. In Japan, there is a very useful expression which symbolises the difficulty of entering a new situation: 'the threshold is too high'. This is often the case for non-church-goers. We had a friend in inner London who used to describe the first time he went to church: 'I walked up and down the street outside the church,' he told us, 'then when I thought no-one was looking, I nipped inside.'

Regular visiting and interchange with parents can help 'lower the threshold' and make the actual physical coming to church more manageable. Still, it is advisable to begin with a social activity, possibly a barbecue or party in the church hall. Why not have a wander around the church at the same time so that if ever the family does come to church, it is not totally unfamiliar to them?

Above all, when planning a service to which non-church-goers are to be invited, plan it from the viewpoint of the visitor. How many 'guest' services have I visited which seem to make no allowance whatsoever for the fact that non-church-goers are present! Apart perhaps from the children's contributions, the remainder of the service follows the normal pattern which often leaves a visitor totally bemused. Careful planning on the other hand with, say, a printed order of service, simple hymns in modern language, an accessible Bible passage, and, where liturgy is used, clear directions to enable the visitor to follow – can all help to make a visitor feel wanted and, if a 'regular' sits next to him, welcomed.

2 It provides opportunities for discussing significant life-related issues with parents, perhaps eventually leading on to spiritual issues. A word of caution here, though. It is a fallacy that parents are reached through their children: it can happen, but statistics, by and large, show that it doesn't. If you are principally involved in children's work with a view to reaching parents, then come out of it: children and parents will soon see where your priorities lie and both will mistrust you. There are other, far more effective avenues to adult involvement.

3 It helps us as group leaders to understand better the children with whom we work. We find that a child will often reproduce family patterns from home within the group. The way in which the child relates to the leader will mirror the way in which she relates to her mother, father, grandparent or other principal caregiver. The way in which she relates to other children in the group will mirror the way in which she relates to her siblings. If she has no brothers or sisters, then depending on the nature of the group, it may well become even more important to her as she seeks to experience in it a sense of family. Parents/caregivers provide important role models to children in numerous ways. If a child

has a negative experience of a role model at home – if, for example, a parent constantly tells her off and belittles her – then she will bring this experience to the group. She then needs the compensating experience of an affirming group leader to provide a positive role model. If we are aware of the family situation of the child, it will help us to understand why she reacts as she does in certain situations. We can then compensate as needed by providing positive role models and positive experiences.

4 It means that caregivers have the chance to see who is looking after their children each Sunday morning (or whenever). As Christians, we can never be too careful to be seen to be totally open, honest and above board in our relationships with children. Introduce yourself to parents of new children as soon as possible. Tell them about yourself. If you are going on an outing, having a party or a video evening, visit each home personally, explaining what is going to happen. Parents have a right and a need to know who is looking after their children and what they are doing together. And sad though it is to have to say it, it is probably best never to see a child on her own. Make sure other children, or adults are around, that doors are left open, and that every encounter is open, so that there is never any foundation for an accusation that might come against you.

But keeping channels of communication open applies equally to churched families and indeed to the whole church family. Each week, each month, each quarter, our Sunday groups usually join the adult worshipping community for part of the service or for a special service. In what other contexts do adults join the children? How well do parents and other church members *know* what is actually happening week by week in the children's groups?

Children also need to feel that they are part of a Christian family, an integral part and not just hangers-on or visitors. How seriously has your church taken on board the need for integration between the children's work and the adult worshipping community? An all-age service is certainly a step in the right direction, but what about a weekly recognition of the part the children contribute to the whole church family? How about a slot for sharing what happened on the outing, what was made in the groups that day, answers to prayer, sharing a special project? How about the children leading the service? How about the adults coming in to share an aspect of the Sunday group? The possible approaches are endless, and I'm sure you can see the benefits. For through it, the child will come to a new understanding of her own value, her own worth as a child: 'Sharing in God's family means that I am very important, I am really valuable. Not only does my group leader think I'm important, but so do all those other grown-ups. I don't experience this anywhere else!'

## How do I relate to grown-ups? (Relationship to authority)

The authority figure in the child's world is the adult. She may privately question what the adult does while she is among her peers, but when it comes to the crunch, it is the adult who is right. This happens because a child of this age has to depend on the adult for virtually everything. But what a tremendous responsibility this places on us as one of the adults in the child's world – perhaps the only Christian adult.

Alice Miller, who has written extensively on the causes and effects of child mistreatment and its cost to society, speaks about the value of an 'enlightened witness' (*Banished Knowledge, 1991* p 171 ff). In the context of her work, she is speaking about the adult who sees child abuse and violence for what it is and is willing to speak out against it, despite a silence and refusal to acknowledge it on the part of society as a whole. She maintains that if a child encounters a single 'enlightened witness' who will serve as an advocate for her in the face of suffering and violence, it can change the entire course of her childhood, and subsequently her adult life, for the good.

In our context, a single Christian adult can serve as an 'enlightened witness'. Such an adult, if she has the ability to become like a child and enter the child's world, is in a unqiue position to serve as a witness to the life-changing quality of a friendship with Jesus. The child may never have another opportunity to experience first-hand the difference that a friendship with Jesus can make to a person's life.

As a group leader or children's worker, you may be the only Christian adult with whom the child ever comes into contact. Children today desperately need 'enlightened witnesses' of this sort to touch their lives. As an aside, we can also serve as the other type of 'enlightened witness': if we earn the trust of the child, we may also hear her confidences, and sensitively and prayerfully decide how we need to respond to them.

As 'enlightened witnesses', we are also tremendously privileged because we are in a unique positon to be a true, trustworthy adult friend to the child. In effect, we are 'being Jesus' for that child. The way we conduct our group, the way we listen, the way we respond, the way we joke, the way we discipline, the way we open up ourselves, enables the child to begin to see Jesus.

'Being in awe of an adult friend or of a distant hero is a first step in learning worship. Being worthy of such adulation is not easy, but it is important,' says Andrew Lester, speaking about children's needs. 'When children find an adult whom they can trust with their innermost thoughts, yet feel accepted and liked anyway, they have found a real treasure' (*Lester 1985*, p 61). Our prayer should be that we can become this kind of treasure, so that the transition to seeing Jesus as an even more wonderful treasure is enabled to happen with ease.

Another adult 'authority' figure to whom children within our church-based children's work relate is the minister or vicar. What is the relationship between your group and the church leadership? Is there frequent interchange, a free back-and-forth relationship? Or does work need to be done, either on your side to structure situations in which the minister can be involved, or on the minister's side to make him/herself more available?

This again relates to the degree of importance placed on children's activities within the church. Where they are seen to be of high priority, ministerial involvement is likely to be greater. It is vital that children feel themselves to be an integral part of the wider church family, and this can be reflected in the level of involvement of the minister with the children's groups. Does the minister make arrangements to visit the groups regularly? Is he a welcome figure? Does he take the trouble to learn the names of group members? Does he know about their families? Is he able to chat naturally and informally? Certainly, not every church leader is a 'natural' with children, but children will respect it if he makes a genuine effort to get to know them.

And if the fault for lack of involvement lies with the children's work leaders, then attempts need to be made to redress this by giving the minister an open invitation to visit the group or by inviting him/her to contribute specifically one week. Children quickly pick up the welcome there is (or isn't!) for them among the adult members of the church. Church leaders can set the tone for this welcome and thereby let children know that real family and real worship is about all age groups being together.

## How do I see my world? (World view)

A child's world view is wonderfully integrated. As already observed, there is no distinction between the material and the spiritual: one aspect of life flows into the next. As we present the Christian faith to children, so we need to take on board where they are coming from and ensure that we do not box in this faith so that it becomes 'that which we do on Sunday (or whichever day) at our group'. Rather, the children need to experience a friendship with Jesus as a relationship which flows through all of life and can touch every aspect of their daily lives.

Thus, we need to explore what it means to be a friend of Jesus at school, at home, in the playground, at the recreation ground, at a friend's house. Within our groups, this can often be brought home by means of role play. It is fine to talk about situations, but that keeps it 'out there'. Inviting the children to 'do' a situation, to act it out and thus get inside the feelings surrounding a given situation, can really help to bring a point home. Don't forget, children recall 90 per cent of what they do, but only 10 per cent of what they hear.

If you do not feel confident doing drama with the children, role-plays need not fill you with dread. What you are actually doing is simply telling the children what part you want them to play and the rest is up to them: words, actions, expressions, sounds. Children can be wonderfully creative and I often come away amazed at what comes out in a role play. Thus, for example, you ask Matthew and Sophie to pretend they are a nine-year-old brother and a six-year-old sister arguing over a television programme. Then you ask them to play the parts again, this time providing a solution they think would make Jesus happy. You will be amazed at the inventiveness that is displayed! It is usually a good idea to give them a few moments to come out of role and remember who they really are and where they are, otherwise you may feel you have gained two new group members.

It is also important, when thinking about how a child views her world, to remember that at this age most things are accepted at face value. A child tends to accept the teaching we give without questioning or challenging it – unless it happens to be strongly challenged elsewhere, for example by a parent. A child can then be very dogmatic and argumentative. Nevertheless this does place

a tremendous responsibility on us as group leaders. What do we give to our group? Are we offering them truths which are really life-changing and meaningful? Or are we just giving them pat answers, reeling off the stories or themes which are in our resource book without first thinking them through ourselves and making them our own?

Another point to remember is that just as a child of this age accepts things at face value, so at this stage, faith will probably belong to them because it belongs to you. This is not always the case as some children of this age do make a conscious choice to own their faith for themselves. But, by and large, the owning for themselves stage will not come until later. This is fine. If a child has seen the value and reality of it for you now, then the movement to their owning it later will be that much easier.

## How is my spiritual side touched? (Use of symbols)

We have already noted that symbols are a very powerful medium of communication with children. Their power lies in the fact that, for a child, they are what they represent. Their meaning doesn't need to be explained. In fact, an explanation can often detract from the symbol because the meaning may be too hard for a child to grasp. However, awe and wonder come naturally to a child and we must not underestimate how God can speak through a symbol and touch the spirit of a child in a profound way.

In sharing communion, whether watching or participating, it is not necessary for a child to understand and think about the full significance of the bread and wine. The knowledge that it is about sharing a meal as Jesus shared a meal with his friends and that he told us to do the same, can be enough.

In the same way, a child can be touched and moved by just watching a baptism. She may not understand what is happening beyond realising that water has to do with washing (which she does each day) and making things grow (like her window box). But the music, the attitude of the grown-ups, the 'out-of-the-ordinary-ness' of it all will touch her sense of the numinous – her sense of the 'other-worldly'.

Symbols do not just have to be what we call 'religious' in order to reach a child, for a child does not naturally make our adult distinction between sacred and secular. As already noted, life is a wholeness, a unity. Thus, the use of colour, of light, of music, of natural objects, can all serve as symbols for the child, touching her sense of awe and wonder and providing a channel for God to reach through.

On another level, what does the atmosphere of your room have to say about awe and wonder, about God's delight in his world, about his love of beauty and order? What does your room symbolise about God to the child? On a day when your room is not being used, go and sit in the centre of it: imagine you are a child and feel its atmosphere, its smell, see its colours, touch the hard and soft objects, hear the surrounding noises. How does it feel to you as a child? What would you like to change?

Now become an adult again and get out a notebook and pencil and write down the things you as a child would like to change. Probably not all of them will be possible or affordable, but some certainly will be – even a vase of flowers! Now go to your cupboard and sort out all the bits and pieces that are not needed or are too old. Have you just been making do? Can you really not afford some felt tip pens that work? And what do those old, torn books say to your children about how you value them? Is it not possible to put up some bright, cheery curtains in place of those drab, colourless ones? And what about a coat of paint? Remember, the atmosphere of the room symbolises the value you place on your children and on your position as group leader.

Finally, for a child, awe and wonder do not just have to do with quietness and meditation. Sometimes they might. But at other times, a child's spiritual side may be so touched that she just wants to bubble over with praise, with excitement, with fun, with happiness. We need to allow that to happen as well. We need to avoid structuring our session so carefully and tightly that we not only don't allow for anything to go wrong, we don't allow the Holy Spirit to play any part either! We need to allow space as appropriate for the children to experience awe and wonder and to express their response to it in a natural and uninhibited way. And if we, too, can become like children, we will be able to enter in and feel their awe and wonder and respond to it.

## Thinkabout

**1** In what ways can you, together with other group leaders, use the 'windows' as a tool in effectively preparing to meet the needs of your group?

**2** How do the different windows through which a child looks at her world, help you as you seek to convey the teachings of Jesus within your group?

**3** For example, how does understanding a child's egocentric approach to the world affect the way in which you communicate Jesus' teaching on Christian living?

**4** For example, how does understanding the way in which a child thinks, combined with an understanding of the child's wider world, affect the way in which you communicate a Bible story?

**5** For example, how does an understanding of the way in which a child views authority figures affect the way in which you conduct your group?

**6** For example, how does an understanding of the family system of a particular child affect the way in which you respond to that child both within your group and outside it?

# PART IV

## Let's put it all together

– Thinking about our responsibility as adults –

*Growth towards God means turning right round and becoming small enough to negotiate with God who is child-size.*    John Davies

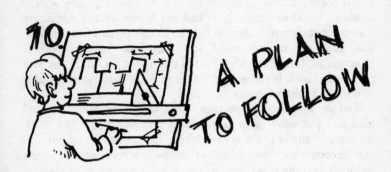

# 10. A PLAN TO FOLLOW

A major event occurred in our family this year: we had a granny annexe built. Grandma was able to move out of our sitting room into her own self-contained area. We all enjoyed a big stretch and breathed sighs of relief – not least Grandma! I learned a lot as I watched the annexe grow day by day and I was struck by how well the experience could be applied to what we do with our children.

Long before any earth was turned, the architect came to draw up plans. We told him we wanted a granny annexe, showed him where it was to go and gave him a general idea as to what we wanted inside. That was it. Because he was skilled in drawing up plans, he went away and drew up his recommendations as to how it should be built, based on his knowledge of what granny annexes are generally like and his knowledge of what our specific Grandma was like. So he recommended certain types of windows, a particular type of roofing, he recommended levels of insulation and a certain type of heating, he suggested using special bricks and an easy-care guttering. He thought about how the annexe would fit in with the remainder of the house and how it would affect the neighbours. Then he handed over the plans to the builders to follow, and they used their many skills to make the granny annexe become a reality. The granny annexe would never have happened had we not had both the architect and the builders.

As children's workers or Sunday group leaders, we are like the architect and the builders all rolled into one. When we talk about learning to enter the world of the child and responding to a child appropriately, and when we talk about being sensitive to the innate spirituality of children, we are talking about learning to develop a *child-centred attitude*. If our architect hadn't had a 'granny annexe attitude', in other words, if he had not known all the distinctive features that were necessary to help an elderly person feel comfortable, then the annexe would have been less than appropriate. Learning to develop a child-centred attitude as set out in the first part of this book is essential if we are to be as effective as possible in our work with children.

And an attitude is more than just a skill to be taken out and used and put away again (although it may well begin like that). Rather an attitude is a way of thinking and a way of seeing things that becomes part and parcel of us. So, for example, we don't suddenly become child-centred on entering our group at church. Our child-centred attitude permeates our whole life. It automatically responds on behalf of the child whose mother is hitting him outside McDonald's, or on behalf of the child who lives a few doors away and is always hanging around the bus shelter, apparently very lonely.

But what of the builders? The task of our builders was to use their skills to make the granny annexe a reality, so Grandma could enjoy it. Likewise, our task as children's workers is to use our skills within the context of a child-centred approach to enable the child to enjoy a life-long friendship with Jesus. What are these skills? They may be skills in story-telling, in craft work, in planning bridge-building activities, in writing songs, in visiting homes, in creative praying . . . the list is endless.

As we select certain approaches, as we encourage our children to look through certain windows (as we saw in Part III), so different skills come into play. Because of our child-centred attitude, we will more readily know which is the most appropriate and effective skill to use to help a child learn a point or make a connection.

Obviously we will make lots of mistakes (just as our builders mis-hung a door at one point). Sometimes these will be because of lapses in our child-centred attitude. It can be very exhausting

*We will make lots of mistakes just as our builders mis-hung a door.*

to re-think our world from a child's viewpoint.

My son is very good at tidying up his bedroom – every two months! Following the Great Day, his room slowly but perceptibly degenerates into chaos, and the floor space gradually disappears as the tide of papers, books, 'makings' and clothes advances. By the end of the first month, I am getting fraught. By the middle of the second month, I am making loud noises, then I stop and think (sometimes): tidiness is obviously not an important issue for him in his world at his age. Why should *I* make it an all-important contentious issue? A tidy room is obviously my adult-centred need, not his child-centred one. Certainly, he needs to know how I feel and as I respect his world, he too needs to respect mine. And he needs to see that one of the benefits of keeping his room tidy is that he can find things. But by adopting a child-centred attitude, I can be more understanding of his clutter.

Sometimes our mistakes will be because of gaps in our skills. Often such gaps can be filled quite easily, perhaps by joining a skills-based training day on games or drama, music or craft. At other times, we might be able to fill the gaps at home, for example, as we pore over craft books or game books for children, or as we practise story-telling or using puppets in front of a mirror.

Sometimes our mistakes will be because we are not yet fully confident as to which is the best skill to use to make a particular

113

point. Thus, if our aim is to show the group that sometimes it is hard to follow Jesus, is this best brought out through a game, a role play, a story or a craft activity? Sometimes there is no 'best' way as such, and this is when we need to go back to our 'windows', to think about how the child views things. We need mentally to go around each member of our group, think about his or her needs and where he or she is coming from (a child–centred attitude), and then select an approach based on the needs of our group.

## Thinkabout

**1** Developing a child-centred attitude does not happen over-night. What areas do you need to work on in order to develop this?

**2** What child-centred skills do you particularly need to develop? What steps will you take to ensure you gain these skills? Training days? Reading? Meeting with other leaders?

# 11. SAND, CEMENT AND STONES

So, thanks to our architect and the builders, our granny annexe was now a reality. But a look at the garden told us that the job wasn't yet finished: it looked like a building site. There were stones, mud and bare patches everywhere. We needed a path, so we decided to lay some crazy paving. Carefully, Frank and Martin laid out odd-shaped slabs of paving in the form of a path. But it was getting late and they had to go home. When they had gone my daughter rushed out and tippy-toed from stone to stone:

'Is this it, Mum? Have they finished?'

'What do you think?'

'Well, all the stones are wobbly and you can pick them up. It's not a very good path!'

Well, of course, Frank and Martin returned the next day and a combination of sand and cement made the mortar which has kept the stones firmly in position ever since.

These truths we have learned about children, these skills we have thought about, the windows we have looked through – all are like the paving stones that made up our new path. Some were little, some big, some less important, others more so. But on their own, they would not have made a solid, stable path. What was needed was the mortar between them to hold them in place.

In the same way, our 'stones' need mortar between them, and just as Frank and Martin's mortar was made up of a combination of sand and cement, so our 'mortar' is made up of two elements. The first is us as leaders, who we are and where our Christian commitment is at. The second element is the Christian faith which we teach and its biblical content. Our 'stones' – a child-centred attitude and child-based skills – may be excellent, but unless, under the guidance of the Holy Spirit, they are held in place by the mortar of our own faith linked with a strong biblical foundation, the stones will wobble and the path will be unstable. However, if stones and mortar are firmly in place, then look what we give the child: a secure path to walk on to an even deeper understanding of what it means to be a follower of Jesus.

This provides a continual challenge to us as leaders. Where do we stand in terms of our own individual faith? Do we struggle? How important to us is prayer and a regular meeting with God through the Bible? From where do we draw our support? How committed are we to praying for our children? Do we have other Christian friends with whom we can share personal concerns? Concerns about our children?

Allied to this, what is our involvement with other church-based children's groups and leaders? Do we meet regularly with other

*'Read the small print, the thinking that underlies the material we use.'*

Sunday group leaders to pray, plan and prepare? If we have to miss worship on a regular basis, how do we compensate for this? Where does our children's group feature in our list of priorities? Have we dried up in our work with children? Do we need a break? How will we achieve this and find spiritual refreshment as well? Who can we approach about this?

Let us also look again at the biblical content of the material we use. Read the editorial pages, the small print, the thinking that underlies the approach. Does the material reflect the truth that, within the Bible and demonstrated through Jesus Christ, we can find a purpose for living and enjoy a restored and eternal friendship with Jesus Christ which begins here and now? More than that, does the material adopt a child-centred approach to communicating these truths? As Bible-centred as the content may be, you still need a child-centred approach for material to be fully effective. Likewise, a child-centred approach without a strong biblical base is only half the story.

These days, in our approach to church resource material for children, we have tried to move away from the school ethos, as this carries negative overtones for many children. Thus, we avoid Sunday 'school', we avoid speaking of 'lessons' and 'pupils', we avoid 'curriculum', we avoid 'classes' and 'teachers'. If your experience of school has been one of boredom, of alienation, if you were a non-book person, or a non-academic, if a job rather than an education was a priority in your family, then traditional Sunday 'school' terms can be less than helpful, especially if compared with the relatively informal group setting to be found in many primary schools today.

However, discarding such terms does not mean we need to throw out the baby with the bath water. There are many encouragements in the Bible to teach or instruct our children (eg, Deuteronomy 6:6ff). Just because we may choose to use different words (eg, 'learn together') does not mean we abdicate our responsibility to instruct. We now have a generation of teenagers – not to mention adults – who are largely ignorant of the Christian faith. We need to do our part to ensure that this does not happen in succeeding generations.

I personally do not believe it is the task of state-run day schools to instruct in the Christian faith with a view to seeking a Christian commitment (nor do most schools have the committed Christians to do so). Certainly it is right to teach Christianity as a major world religion, and, recognising that we are a country with Christian foundations, to give it the primacy due to it. However, we must also accept and respect that we are now a multi-race, multi-faith society, and recognise that a day school is not the appropriate forum for seeking a commitment to Christ. Where this must happen is in our homes and in our church-based children's groups.

It is true that 'Sunday' groups principally attract children of church-going parents, but they, too, need a strong foundation, and friendships with Christian adults outside the home. And if 'Sunday' groups are not appropriate for a non-church-going child, then we need to set up week-night clubs which can exist in their own right or may also serve as a bridge into a 'Sunday' group.

Above all, we need to be faithful to our calling to be children's workers. God's commands in Deuteronomy 6:5 are so positive: 'Love the Lord your God with all your heart, with all your soul, and with all your strength'. And the writer goes on to say, 'Teach them to your children ... at home, when away, when resting, when working.' And, by extension, 'Whatever you do, don't forget them, even if you have to attach them to your person or write them up around your house.' There is a real sense of urgency here, a passionate urgency. Do we sense that same urgency when we work with our children? Do we love God with our whole being and can we, therefore, enter into his love for children – children who are hurting, who are joyful, who are abused, who are privileged, who are damaged, who are content? As we become like a child, so we learn to understand God's love for children.

## Thinkabout

**1** How much importance do you place on maintaining the vitality of your own faith as you work with children? How can you enter into God's love for children?

**2** What importance does your church place on having a regular meeting to pray and plan for the children's work? What can you do to ensure this takes place?

**12.**

**TO DAD FROM EMMA**

Hello Dad.
Today is church day.
Nan said did I want to go to church?
I said yes, 'cause there wasn't
anything good on telly.
We saw a dog with a hurt leg come down the road
I wanted to pat him
Nan said not to 'cause he might bite me.
It was all dark inside the church
And cold.
It was like that place we went to
When Grandad died
The place with the curtain
It smelt cold, too.
This man was giving out books to
people.
He didn't give me one even though I
stared at him hard to make him.
Richard told me if you stare hard at
someone, you can make them
do what you want.

He said it was something to do
with a hippo.
There was this man at the front
in a long dress
Or maybe it was a woman
Or an angel.
I asked Nan was it an angel
but she told me be quiet and listen.
You're supposed to have angels in
churches, aren't you?
The angel told everyone to open
their books.
I hadn't got one, so I didn't.
(Or maybe it's God)
Yesterday me and Bonnie picked
dandelions in the rec.
I got stung by these nettles
They was under the climbing frame.
It hurts on my leg.
I said to Nan could we go now?
I was cold
She said shh.
Everyone stood up and started singing.
This fly was crawling up the
cushion on the floor,
I kicked it with my foot
It flew off.
I thought wouldn't it be funny if it landed on the
angel's nose.
Then the angel said for all the
children to go out.
Nan pushed me and said to go,
So I did.
I didn't want to
I didn't know anyone
I wanted to stay with Nan,
But it was boring in church
And cold.
We went down this hall with green walls,
There wasn't many children
They stared at me.

Then this lady took my hand
Her smile made her eyes all crinkle up
She smelt like Auntie Rose.
She said what was my name?
and I said Emma.
She said, I'm Sally.
We all sat on the carpet
It was brown with yellow bits in it
Like those dandelions.
My leg hurt on the carpet.
I sat next to this boy called Gary.
He gave me an orange chew.
I ate it, then I thought
Would Miss tell me off like in school?
I had to stand on the black line
Yesterday –
Sam and me was chewing jelly tots
Miss saw me,
She didn't see him
It wasn't fair.
On the carpet we all shared news.
I said about the hurt dog and how Nan
said it might bite.
Sally said she's got a dog.
Sally has a monkey puppet
His name is Jacko.
Jacko told us about how Jesus
made this sick lady well
I thought of mum.
I asked Jacko did he like Jesus
He said yes and that Jesus was
very special.
Christmas is Jesus' birthday
Miss said that at school.
I want a new bike for Christmas
Like Katie's
Or roller skates.
Sally prayed to Jesus
Like Mr Russell does in assembly
Only different.
She asked Jesus to help Alan learn

his spellings
Mr Russell never asks things like that at school.
Is Jesus and Father Christmas the same?
That angel probably knows,
Sally probably knows, too,
She was talking to Jesus like she knew him.
Sally said the group was going round
her house
After school on Friday
For a party.
She said could I go –
Dad, can I?
Can I?
Nan said we'll see,
I guess that means no
Please Dad?
I like Sally.
She understood when I said about the dog.
She understood when I said about the cold church
She said she gets cold there, too.
We made these gold star badges.
I stuck the pin on the back myself
With sticky tape
It says Jesus.
Sally says that's 'cause he's special.
I'll show it you when I get home
Please, Dad, can I go?
Can I?
Please?

Love from Emma

# And finally. . .

So we discuss and write our adult noises about these things. I hope one day, however, that I shall have grown young enough to accept all this without so much argument. As J M Barrie's character said, 'I'm not young enough to know everything.'
*John Davies*

**Dad** (in response to daughter's comment): That's not right.
**Emma:** But I know everything.
**Dad:** Oh no, you don't.
**Emma:** But God knows everything.
**Dad:** But you're not God.
**Emma:** No, but I'm a friend of God.

# References

Wendy Body, 'In my view . . .', *Child Education* (Scholastic Publications, October 1989).

Archibald D Hart, *Stress and Your Child* (Word, 1992).

*How Faith Grows: Faith Development and Christian Education* (National Society/Church House Publishing, 1991).

Andrew D Lester, *Pastoral Care with Children in Crisis* (Westminster Press, 1985).

Alice Miller, *Banished Knowledge* (Virago, 1991).

Walter Wangerin, *The Manger is Empty* (HarperSanFrancisco, 1989).

Macrina Wiederkehr, *A Tree Full of Angels* (HarperCollins, 1990).

D W Winnicott, *The Family and Individual Development* (Tavistock Publications, 1965).

William Wordsworth, 'Ode: Intimations of Immortality from Recollections of Early Childhood', *Norton Anthology of English Literature* (W W Norton, 1966).

# Further Resources

## Books about understanding children and how they think

Coles, Robert. *The Spiritual Life of Children* (HarperCollins, 1990) – talking and listening to children and entering their world.

Cully, Iris V. *Christian Child Development* (Gill and Macmillan, 1980) – combining psychological and religious aspects of growth.

Donaldson, Margaret. *Children's Minds* (Fontana, 1978) – a classic on the development of children's thinking.

Donaldson, Margaret, Robert Grieve, Chris Pratt, Eds. *Early Childhood Development and Education* (Blackwell, 1983) – how children develop, think and communicate.

Fowler, James. *Stages of Faith: The Psychology of Human Development and the Quest for Meaning* (Harper & Row, 1981) – theories as to how faith develops.

Hart, Archibald D. *Stress and Your Child: Know the Signs and Prevent the Harm* (Word, 1992) – a practical book on caring for children.

*How Faith Grows* (General Synod Board of Education, National Society, 1991) – the development of faith in the context of Christian education.

Hughes, Jeremie. *Will my Rabbit go to Heaven?* (Lion, 1981) – questions children ask.

Lester, Andrew D. *Pastoral Care with Children in Crisis* (Westminster Press, 1985) – prioritising care for the younger members of the church family.

Lurie, Alison. *Not in Front of the Grown-ups: Subversive Children's Literature* (Cardinal, 1990) – a stimulating look at children's books.

Miller, Alice. *Banished Knowledge* (Virago, 1991) – a challenging look at the effects of child-rearing.

Sylva, Kathy and Ingrid Lunt. *Child Development – A First Course* (Blackwell, 1982) – a basic introduction to child development.

Weber, Hans Reudi. *Jesus and the Children: Bible Resources for Study and Preaching* (World Council of Churches, 1979) – a scholarly account of Jesus' attitude to children.

Westerhoff III, John W. *Will Our Children Have Faith?* (Dove Communications, 1976) – thinking about the growth of faith in a Christian community.

Westerhoff III, John W. *Bringing up Children in the Christian Faith* (Winston Press, 1980) – sharing faith with your children.

## Books about children within a church setting

*All God's Children: Children's Evangelism in Crisis* (General Synod Board of Education, National Society, 1991) – our priorities for those outside the church.

Bridger, Francis. *Children Finding Faith* (Scripture Union, 1988) – insights into how children find faith.

Butler, Paul. *Reaching Children* (Scripture Union, 1992) – making Jesus known to children.

Crawford, Kathleen. *Under Fives Welcome!* (Scripture Union, 1990) – practical ideas for working with under fives in church.

Graystone, Peter. *Help! There's a Child in my Church!* (Scripture Union, 1989) – practical ideas for working with 7 to 11s.

Graystone, Peter and Eileen Turner. *A Church for All Ages* (Scripture Union, 1993) – practical approaches to all-age worship.

## Resource Books

*Children's Arts and Crafts and More Children's Arts and Crafts* (Australian Women's Weekly) – available from newsagents and supermarkets – published by Australian consolidated Press, 54 Park Street, Sydney, NSW 2000.

Einon, Dorothy. *Creative Play* (Penguin, 1986) – play with a purpose from birth to ten years.

Gibson, Ray, et al. *Things to Make with Paper* (Usborne, 1992).

Goodland, Patrick. *Over 300 Games for All Occasions* (Scripture Union, updated 1992).

Green, Rachel. *Over 120 Quizzes for All Occasions* (Scripture Union, 1980).

Pinchbeck, Lesley. *Theme Games* (Scripture Union, 1993).

*Child Education* (Scholastic Publications, Ltd, Westfield Road, Southam, Leamington Spa, Warks. CV33 0JH) – a monthly resource magazine for teachers working with primary school children containing excellent ideas, cover price: £2.10, annual subscription: £25.20. Scholastic also publish resource titles for teachers such as *Bright Ideas* and *Inspirations*, which can be adapted for church settings; catalogue available on request.

*Bodybuilders, the J Team* (Scripture Union) – holiday club material.

SALT programme – *Sharing and Learning Together* – Bible-based, child-centred resources for use in churches, published quarterly by Scripture Union; includes leader's magazine and children's activity material

   *SALT:  3 to 4+ and Sparklers*
   *SALT:  5 to  7+ and All Stars*
   *SALT:  8 to 10+ and Trailblazers*
   *SALT: 11 to 13+ and Lazer*
   *SALT: All Ages* – for family services and adult worship
      PLUS
   *You're Only Young Once*: undated material for over 13s